Justin Martyr
on
Baptism and Eucharist:

Texts in Translation with
Introduction and Commentary

by
Colin Buchanan

Church of England Bishop, Retired

Contents

* *Most of Justin's texts presented here are only parts of chapters. But those marked with an * are complete chapters.*

Translation, Introduction and Commentary copyright Colin Buchanan 2007

THE COVER PICTURE
Justin Martyr as portrayed by Andre Thevet,
Les Vrais Pourtraits et Vies Hommes Illustres, 1584.
Special Collection Library, University of Michigan.

First Impression December 2007

ISSN 0951-2667
ISBN 978-1-85311-905-7

Foreword

This Series of Joint Studies has, in tandem with the old Grove Liturgical Studies, now completed 33 years of continuous publication, providing 112 titles thus far. Both Series have featured liturgical texts from the patristic era, translated and introduced in a format accessible to students, and moderately priced. The first text was Geoffrey Cuming's *Hippolytus: A Text for Students* (Grove Liturgical Study no.8) in December 1976, and, as with all the patristic texts, it has remained in print throughout the period. But, as this range has grown, a key patristic author, earlier in date than any in the Series, has been missing, namely Justin Martyr. Justin was a gleam in my eye when I retired three years ago, and I am grateful to the Joint Editorial Board for commissioning this Study on him. I have been further stimulated by the far-reaching and magisterial treatment of Justin by Paul Bradshaw in *The Search for the Origins of Christian Worship* (2nd ed., SPCK, 2002) and *Eucharistic Origins* (Alcuin/SPCK, 2004). Paul Bradshaw has gone beyond the stimulus of his books and has helped me in person, even when I have queried his conclusions; and I am very grateful.

At an early stage, I was enormously helped by attending in July 2006 a conference on Justin convened by the Centre for Study of Christian Origins of Edinburgh University. Most speakers barely touched on Justin's liturgical evidence, but their papers provided valuable contextual material. I myself read a coat-trailing paper 'Justin Martyr: Questions liturgists would like to ask him'. That set out much of the ground to be surveyed, and is now published within the scholarly symposium of the conference's papers: Sara Parvis and Paul Foster (eds), *Justin Martyr in his Worlds* (Fortress Press, Minneapolis, 2007). Those questions which I asked are, inevitably, present-day ones; and they defy easy answers, as Justin was unaware of what liturgists might later ask. Nevertheless, this present Study has to address the questions and nudge its way towards answers. One can hardly be innovative with patristic evidence - but I have endeavoured not simply to repeat well-worn affirmations of others, but to look afresh at the message of this fascinating martyr-apologist.

My Introduction is intended to draw together evidence of Justin's thought overall, while many issues of detail appearing only once in the texts are covered in the later commentary on the actual texts.

Colin Buchanan

1. Introduction

A. Justin Martyr – the man in his times

Justin Martyr lived from early in the second century to his martyrdom around 165 AD. His extant writings are his dialogue with the Jew Trypho (called *Dialogue* hereafter) and the two books of his *apologia* to the emperor Antoninus (of which the first and substantial book is called *Apology* and cited as '*Apol.*' hereafter, and the second is carefully identified when mentioned). Justin is a Samaritan (*Dial.* 120), but, perhaps typically of Samaritans in his time, acknowledges himself uncircumcised. Therefore, in relation to Trypho, he is a Gentile, identifying himself with Gentile uncircumcised Christians (e.g. in *Dial.*123). and stressing the otiose character of outward circumcision.[1] However, his Samaritan background has deeply versed him in the Old Testament, as his Christian foreground has in the Christian story. He describes himself as a philosopher, one whom contemporary pagan philosophy did not satisfy, and this has led him to Christ. Modern commentators call him a layman, an interesting feature of a theological writer in a period when we might have expected bishops to be the teachers of the faith. However, he does not call himself 'lay' in terms we would recognize, for, because he does not mention bishops or presbyters of any sort, the distinction involved in our word 'lay' is nowhere in sight.[2]

Eusebius places Justin's *Dialogue* in Ephesus in the 130s[3], which tallies with Trypho's own report that he had 'escaped from the war lately carried on there [sc. in Judaea]'(*Dial.*1), which would refer to the Bar Cochba revolt, after which a Jewish resident of Judaea might well become a refugee. However, we cannot easily locate the whole work then, as in *Dial.*35 Marcionites are classified with others as impious and heretical. Marcion originated in Pontus (*Apol.*7), but went to Rome around 140, and was excommunicated for his heretical teaching in 144.[4] Thus, even if the *Dialogue* is dramatically located in Ephesus in the 130s, its final

---

[1] Trypho tells him to get circumcised (*Dial.*8), and he at a different point responds 'What need have I to be circumcised?' (*Dial.*29). See also the discussions about circumcision on pp.16-17 and 33-35 below.

[2] Justin's account of baptism in *Apol.*61 locates him among the group from the church performing the baptism, and this and his teaching role (see *Acts of Martyrdom*, p.32 below) may indicate he held a respected position in the local assembly.

[3] Eusebius *HE* IV.18.6

[4] The actual heretics named here are the *Marcianoi*, a unique term, but it must mean followers of Marcion (not least as grouped with Valentinians and Basilidians). None were rampant in Ephesus in the 130s, but they have anachronistically invaded the text *as published*. *Marcianoi* may be a textual corruption of *Marcionoi*.

publication must be dated later, probably in Rome, and indeed after the *Apology,* as *Dial.*120 refers to *Apol.*26: 'When I held communication with Caesar, I said that [the Samaritans] were deceived by Simon Magus.' Yet if, as I hesitantly propound, a genuine Ephesian provenance in the 130s lies behind his text of the latter 150s, the odd anachronism need not affect that attribution. The *Dialogue* is replete with Old Testament quotations, as Justin zealously strives to demonstrate that those scriptures on which he and Trypho are both agreed actually portray Jesus Christ, and a new covenant in Christ.[5] His zeal carries him into a vast range of typology, some of it frankly fanciful.

The *Apology* belongs to Rome in the reign of the emperor Antoninus Pius (138-161) and is generally dated in the early 150s.[6] The *Second Apology* may be a little later. Justin's philosophical background comes to the fore (though his citation of scripture is also present) as he labours to bring the fact and the facts of Christianity before the pagan emperor. The *Apology* has been much visited by liturgists, as chapters 61 and 65-67 give the fullest extant description of Christians at worship from the whole of the first two centuries.

Because Justin never mentions bishops of Rome (or bishops of any sort), it is hard to relate him and his writings to the bishops of his time, Pius (c140-155), and Anicetus (c155-167).[7] Other writings of Justin, while mentioned by him in the *Apology* and listed by Eusebius, are not extant, and our access to his evidence of second century church life is confined to the *Dialogue* and the *Apology.* Yet these two writings provide substantial and amazingly complementary sources – for not only is Justin among the very earliest of extant post-apostolic writers, but, while other writers largely addressed other Christians, Justin provides a unique combination of early commendations of the Christian faith to a Jew and a pagan respectively.[8] If on *a priori* grounds we would have expected such

---

[5]   There is a slightly relaxed and even smiling interchange in *Dial.*58, where Justin declares he is utterly artless in his presentation, and Trypho in effect tells him now to pull the other leg.

[6]   Justin himself reckoned in *Apol.*46 'Christ was born one hundred and fifty years ago'.

[7]   The succession in Eusebius matches that in Irenaeus, *Adv.Haer.*III.3, but is probably not independent, but derived from Irenaeus. The dating just enables Polycarp's visit to debate the date of Easter with Anicetus to be reckoned as 155. Peter Lampe's magisterial treatment gives only a shadowy role to any bishop in Rome in relation to disparate and relatively independent congregations at that time (see, P.Lampe, *From Paul to Valentinus: Christians at Rome in the First Two Centuries* (ET, Fortress, USA, 2003) pp.403f.).

[8]   Sara Parvis, partly through dating other apologists later than Justin, securely concludes '...it was Justin himself who forged the genre of Christian apologetic ... We are therefore at liberty to consider Justin the first Christian apologist.' (Parvis/Foster, *op.cit*, pp.117 and 122). But Paul Parvis reminds us that Justin himself does not use the term '*apologia*', but instead reckons he is presenting a 'petition' to the authorities (*op.cit*. p.26).

accounts to be reticent about the conduct of semi-secret Christian assemblies, we will welcome all the more his actual accounts, especially in the *Apology*, which far exceed those expectations.

Betrayed by an enemy, Crescens, Justin was martyred early in Marcus Aurelius' reign (161-180), probably around 165. The *Acts of Martyrdom*, an anonymous work usually treated as reliable, reports from Justin a few further words of *apologia*. These bear, at least obliquely, upon our themes and so are included here. The martyrdom gave added weight to his writings – he was remembered with pride and his works read and handed on by his own student, Tatian, and by Irenaeus, thus leading to his pre-eminent place in Book IV of Eusebius.

B. Text, selection and translation

Our texts of Justin stem from a single manuscript, *Parisinus Graecus 450*, dated to 1364, and located in the National Library in Paris. This lay behind the first printed edition of Justin of Stephanus in Paris in 1551, and subsequent editions all spring from the same source. So there are no variant readings requiring an editor's discriminatory judgment, though at points the manuscript may itself be corrupt or defective – and then conjectural amendments have to be weighed. One slight complication is that a variant manuscript of *Apol.*65-67, known nowadays as Codex Bobbonianus and located in Rome, apparently antedates the 1551 edition, and it, or a comparable or dependent manuscript copy of those chapters, was known in England immediately prior to 1551 – and was cited in dispute by both Cranmer and Gardiner.[9] There is conjecture also as to how the *Second Apology* relates to the *First Apology* (which it preceded in the manuscript and the early editions); but that does not bear upon the liturgical evidence and need not delay us here.[10]

Obviously, Justin was not writing for historians of liturgy, and his liturgical material, whether by passing reference or more connected account, is embedded in discourse and argument which he marshalls for totally other purposes. I have selected passages a little beyond those normally under liturgists' consideration, and have toothcombed much previous scholarly

---

[9] See the Parker Society Cranmer volume 1, *On the Lord's Supper*, pp.143 and 263. The Bobbonianus manuscript bears on the issue of whether Justin's wine was in fact water – see pp.22 and 45 below - but it was judged 'very faulty' by A.W.F.Blunt in 1911 and is reliably reckoned an inaccurate copy of those chapters from *Parisinus Graecus 450*, not an independent source.

[10] It is wonderfully handled by Paul Parvis in his chapter 'Justin, Philosopher and Martyr: The Posthumous Creation of the Second Apology' in Parvis/Foster, *op.cit.*, pp.22-37. His title betrays his (tentative) conclusion, but his 15 pages of brilliantly illustrated close argument indicate the complexity of the problem.

discussion to ensure that all relevant material is available within this one Study. The passages are necessarily lifted from their original contexts, though, where the larger context may bear upon our understanding, 1 have sought to indicate that. Handling Justin's thought consistently also requires cross-reference to parts of his writings not reprinted here, a lack which is, 1 fear, inevitable. The selected passages are themselves scattered and hardly connected to each other, so 1 have arranged them thematically. Though the account of baptism in *Apol.*61 runs naturally into the baptismal eucharist in *Apol.*65, yet Justin himself divides the two by a diversion, so the separation of them here may be excusable. However, he helpfully keeps chapters 65-67 together, and that latter vital sequence has been easy to display.

The translation is my own, though obviously fuelled by others. It is fairly literal, to give the closest possible access to the wording, and, usually, the word order, of the Greek. 1 have shunned the tudor language of past translators (who, in the days of the King James Version of the Bible, viewed patristic writings as sacred text requiring comparable English); but 1 have not used 'inclusive' language where it would obscure Justin's meaning. 1 have sought consistency of translation for key words, with transliteration and discussion in the commentary where necessary. Greek originals are rendered in transliterated characters, in the general style of this series.[11]

C. Position in Early Church History

What then are liturgists to make of Justin's fascinating evidence? The question rarely terminates on simply his evidence. Scholars understandably seek to fit Justin into a stream of liturgical history – possibly adjusting the account as they read him, but also reading into him *a priori* ideas about such a stream, imposing on him liturgical components which 'must' have been present in what he describes. This has a certain surface plausibility – liturgical practice easily settles into a repetitive pattern, and a glimpse of practice in one place and time might provide pointers to practice in earlier and later times in that same place, and possibly, though less certainly, to practice elsewhere at the same time. But the 'reading into him' which lies behind assertions of a 'stream' is actually perilous, and the more so in pursuit of some known desirable outcome as the 'practice of the early church'. It is against such venturing that Paul Bradshaw's popularization of the distinction between 'lumpers' and 'splitters' has been directed – the

---

[11]   1 have been in a dilemma concerning numbered sub-headings within the text of each chapter, the origins of which 1 have not traced (they are not in Migne's *Patrologia*). 1 have inserted those 1 could find, but have never invoked them in cross-referencing, and most authors ignore them.

lumpers being scholarly bad guys, who, in terms of my metaphor, assert the continuity and content of such a 'stream', tracing its character back *from later evidence.*[12] This Study's starting point is that the sheer paucity of second century evidence not only allows no access to any such stream in Justin's time, but also gives no ground for asserting any existed then. I offer my own analogy from the Edinburgh symposium:

> 'To inspect the liturgical evidence of the first and second centuries is like flying from Cairo to the Cape in order to get a picture of Africa, only to find that there is thick cloud all the way, with but half a dozen gaps in it. If through those gaps in the cloud we get a hasty glimpse of water on two occasions, of a snow-capped mountain on one, of a desert on one, of a city on one, and of an extensive ostrich farm on one, what have we learned about Africa? Is it one continent or more than one? If it *is* one, is there any geophysical, climatic, zoological, anthropological, or economic relation between the parts? The flight and its six camera-snaps simply will not tell us. Our equivalent in the world of liturgy is to look at Clement of Rome in the late first century (with one or two hints about worship), at Ignatius of Antioch with a few more, at Pliny's Letter with a two-liner, at the *Didache* (which might be the wild card, like my snow-capped mountain in Africa), and then at Justin himself mid-century, before we come to [later authors].'[13]

The absence of evidence from before 200 AD is overwhelming. In Justin we may look back cautiously to see connections with the New Testament – and, where they occur (as, e,g. in the sheer use of baptism and the eucharist), we may hesitantly affirm a dependence upon the initial Christian practice, and possibly a continuity from the very beginning. Where there is discontinuity from the New Testament we can affirm little beyond 'Well, that is how Justin says it was.' There is also a likely tendency, easy to discern but often overlooked by those seeking an apostolic stream of church life, towards 'chinese whispers' – the slow alteration and corruption of the tradition, without any one generation realizing it is altering anything, which may also produce divergence between different places. We cannot know which earlier authors Justin had even seen, let alone followed, but I have cited apparently relevant evidence from them, sometimes simply as illustration, without prejudice to the question whether he did know them.

---

[12] See Paul Bradshaw, *The Search,* pp.ix-x, and Paul Parvis, who writes memorably of 'the temptation to join all possible dots' (Parvis/Foster, *op.cit.* p.32) – an exercise which, in the patristic evidence about liturgy, lacks what our nursery books offer, as in those books *the dots are numbered* - and thus the links prescribed.

[13] From my essay 'Questions liturgists would like to ask Justin Martyr' in Parvis/Foster, *op.cit.,* p.153

If restraint is needed when looking back from Justin to earlier authors, total abstinence is required from any temptation to read back into Justin later practices about which he is silent. The temptation exists, but 'we have no reason to assume there was anything more to the rite [i.e. the eucharist] than Justin is telling us.'[14] Reading back is frankly illicit.[15] The dogmaticians know not to read Chalcedonian orthodoxy into Justin's account of the relationship of Father and Son who are one God. How much less should the liturgists assume that contingent later phenomena of liturgy are there in Justin, but are, so to speak, just beneath the surface? So what later use would anyone want to posit? A preparatory catechumenate before baptism? Prayer over the baptismal water? Baptisms conducted at Easter? Post-baptismal anointings or laying on of hands? The use of the Lord's Prayer in liturgy? An identification of the 'orders' of liturgical ministers? 'Offertory theology'? The use of the narrative of institution in the eucharist? Perhaps even the invocation of saints (especially the BVM)? And what of Dix's 'fourfold shape'? My list deliberately brings together items which have been argued as present (but just out of sight) in Justin and items which, as far as I know, have not been so argued, but with equal force – and equal lack of force – could have been. In Bradshaw's terms, this is the province of 'lumpers', and, as he powerfully demonstrates, they are much to be eschewed.

Bradshaw goes further. In *Eucharistic Origins* he reflects that Justin's description of the eucharist may contain features unlike the expectations aroused by latterday authors, notably Dix, from later uses. These are discussed in their contexts below.[16] But he also further warns: 'what is described by Justin Martyr may not have been observed everywhere at that time.'[17] Here is the splitting at its most potent – if Justin does *not* tell us how the eucharist was widely celebrated in his own time, then (a) nothing can be extrapolated from his account, and (b) we have *no evidence at all* for a general pattern of Christian worship in the second century AD. Bradshaw's conclusion is irrefutable.

[14] Martin Stringer, *The Sociology of Christian Worship* (Cambridge, 2005) p.45.

[15] Thus Joseph Jungmann, to take one instance, has to struggle defensively to show a continuity (which on his premises he undoubtedly needs) between the mass from the fourth century onwards and the second century account given by Justin (*The Mass of the Roman Rite: Its Origins and Development* (ET, Burns and Oates, London, 1959) pp.13-17).

[16] Bradshaw's suggestion that the eucharist may have been celebrated with substantial quantities of food and drink is not discussed here (and is a matter of sheer hypothesizing from the texts). For the idea that it was done with bread and water, see p.22 below. For the idea that there were two separate eucharistic prayers, see p.23 below. Bradshaw's further suggestions that the eucharist was celebrated with bread alone, or with cup and bread in reverse order, do not reflect any part of Justin's works.

[17] Paul Bradshaw, *The Search*, p.139.

Those who read into Justin what is not evidently there may allege that he discreetly dissembles in what he tells the emperor.[18] This is a counsel of despair. Justin tells Trypho that Christians are accused of cannibalism and sexual orgies (*Dial* 10), yet he tells the emperor that they assemble to eat the flesh of Christ (*Apol.* 66). If any report of his could expose believers to genuine misunderstanding, let alone deliberate persecution, the risk-taking in references to eating flesh and drinking blood could hardly be outstripped by anything else. Justin here contrasts with the wretched Bythinians whom Pliny had tortured 50 years earlier, for they had to claim first that they had abandoned the faith 25 years before that, and then that what they had shared as Christians had been innocent ordinary food. Their wriggling defensiveness is wholly understandable, but Justin's *Apology* is quite different – as transparent as possible, confident in relation to Antoninus, and ready to take any risks to which this may expose the author. So, if he tells the emperor about eating the flesh of Christ, at what point should he have concealed something less flagrant?

We should also note that the authority accorded until recently to the *Apostolic Tradition*, supposedly by Hippolytus of Rome, has greatly supported the concept of a 'stream' of liturgical life, preserving apostolic ways. Thus Gregory Dix writes about its baptismal rite 'In its details this represents the practice at Rome in the later second century...But...in its main outlines the rite must be older than...the middle of the second century.'[19] Dix did not attempt here any meshing with Justin's account (the lecture conveniently ignored Justin), but the mindset of 'reading back' (and Dix is ready, with little less certitude, to read back to the apostles themselves) is very clear. It is paralleled by the ways E.C.Ratcliff and Arthur Couratin read Hippolytus' eucharistic prayer back into a long-continued 'stream' of liturgical use (and treat 'confirmation' similarly). Bradshaw, of course, is labelling Dix's famous 'fourfold shape' as itself a 'reading back' in the interests of a theory.[20] But not only is the methodology defective, but in these particular cases it is further disqualified by growing doubts thrown over the *Apostolic Tradition* itself.[21]

---

[18] See, e.g., E.C.Ratcliff's efforts described in the Commentary on p.36 below.

[19] G.Dix, *The Theology of Confirmation in relation to Baptism* (Dacre Press, 1946) p.10.

[20] Paul Bradshaw, *Eucharistic Origins*, pp.vi,12 etc.

[21] Wonderfully characterized by Bryan Spinks: 'This document [*Apostolic Tradition*] was, in the 1960s, regarded as crucial for liturgical renewal. It has now become something of an albatross.' (*Early and Medieval Rituals of Baptism*, Ashgate, 2006, p.28). The determinative conferring of the albatross status occurs in, Paul Bradshaw, Maxwell E.Johnson, and L.Edward Phillips, *The Apostolic Tradition* (Fortress, Minneapolis, 2002).

D Worship Context

(i) Worship of the Assembly

The theme of this Study is Justin's teaching on baptism and eucharist, but we also have a glimpse in *Apol*.13 of the assembly gathered for worship without mention of the eucharist (as in 1 Cor.14?). The chief functions outlined there are prayer (*euche*) and thanksgiving (*eucharistia*), which Justin then describes in the opposite order – first gratitude for benefits received (he *almost* says 'for our creation, preservation and all the blessings of this life'), then petitions to live redeemed lives and inherit eternal life. The communal bonding in this assembly is provided by *pompas kai humnas* – translated as 'solemn prayers and hymns'. In the context Justin also establishes that God the Creator is the prime object of their worship, that Jesus Christ is Son of God and is also worshipped, and that the 'prophetic' Spirit holds third place. All pagan or Jewish ceremonial ('blood and libations and incense') is ruthlessly avoided.

Apol.13 does not mention reading scripture or preaching, but in neighbouring chapters Justin writes of being 'taught by the Word' (i.e. by Jesus Christ), and here he does say Christ is 'our teacher'. In chapter 14 he describes how Christians have been 'persuaded by the word' and thus observe new lifestyles, and have 'learned' (*manthano*) Christ (cf. Eph.4.20), and thus been discipled (*ematheteuthesan*). Teaching in the assembly or informal contexts bonded and purified the church. And, if Justin's own style is at all typical, the teaching was conveyed and reinforced by quotation from scripture throughout, whether or not actual scripture passages were being read aloud. His characterization of the Spirit as '*prophetikon*' also emphasizes the giving and receiving of teaching within the church. *Apol.* 13 thus becomes something of a backdrop to chapters 65 and 67.

(ii) Christ our Great High Priest

In the Epistle to the Hebrews a central theme is the high priesthood of Jesus Christ, with demonstration of his priestly appointment, qualifications and role, and the contrast in these between him and the Levitical priests. This category of thought is unique to Hebrews, and there stems solely from Jesus applying Psalm 110.1 to himself (Matt.22.44), from which the author concludes that Psalm 110.4 equally portrays Christ. Christ then is the priest 'after the order of Melchisedek', with a high priesthood unique to himself, to be neither shared nor superseded. On these two Psalm verses the author builds a weighty doctrinal structure, wholly compatible with, say, Pauline theology, but wholly independent of it in its components. It is Christ as high priest who, having offered the sacrifice of himself and passed 'within the veil', gives the church access to the Father (Heb.4.14-16, 10.19-22), which is the basis for the bidding 'not to forsake the gathering together of yourselves' (10.25), and to 'offer the sacrifice of praise continually' (13.15).

Clearly, post-apostolic Christian authors who label Christ 'high priest' do not necessarily have the whole doctrinal pattern of Hebrews in mind. They are far less specific about Christ's functions as high priest than is Hebrews, and it *could* be that the title was simply one of respect, as Christ now occupied the highest place in Christians' estimation, the supreme being to whom to raise one's hat or bow one's knee.[22] But using the title must have originated in the use of it unique to Hebrews, recurring there in nine successive chapters (2-10), the basis for its theological argument throughout. In fact the title 'high priest' for Jesus Christ is strikingly recurrent through the early literature: in the Letter of Clement to the Corinthians (1 Clem. 36 and 64); in Ignatius of Antioch (*Philadelphians* 9); in Polycarp (*Philippians* 12)[23]; and in the quoted direct speech of Polycarp in *The Martyrdom of Polycarp* 14.[24] At the same time, just as no New Testament writer applies words from the *hiereus* stem to Christian ministers, so, with tiny exceptions, Christian authors generally until around 200AD are similarly - and, in the light of later usage, remarkably - abstinent. One tiny exception is Clement of Rome, who in 40-41 cites Old Testament priestly roles to illustrate varieties of function within the church, and, although he is merely illustrating, a prejudiced commentator can just conclude that he went beyond illustration to identification of Christian ministers as *archiereis* and *hiereis*. Chapter 44 contains the passing phrase about 'those who have offered the gifts of a bishop's office', where 'offering' might suggest a 'priestly' role.[25] In *Didache* 13 prophets are entitled to firstfruits 'for they are your *archiereis*' - but in enjoining substantial support for Christian ministers, its citing as precedent the material support of old covenant priests is hardly surprising (cf. 1 Cor.9.13), and implies nothing about priestly cultic functions in new covenant ministers. Other authors never use the '*hier-*' stem for Christian ministers.

---

[22]   Later exposition emphasized the worldwide scope of Melchisedek's priesthood, as opposed to the limited sphere of the Aaronic - but it also succumbed to a temptation to invoke Melchisedek's 'sacrifice' (as a type of the eucharist with *its* worldwide sphere), for all that Gen. 14 has no mention of a 'sacrifice', and the idea is a wishful extrapolation from his 'priesthood' combined with the mention in Gen.14 of bread and wine. Thus it passed into the old Roman canon.

[23]   Chapter 12 is in the portion only extant in a later Latin translation. The Latin, interestingly, is 'pontifex', which in Latin ran alongside 'magnus sacerdos' and 'summus sacerdos'. It is later found in the Vulgate in the Pentateuch and John's Gospel and regularly in Hebrews.

[24]   Interestingly chapter 21 mentions an earthly 'high priest' - one Philip of Tralles - who from the context is not a Christian minister, but a Jew or even a pagan; and the title can apparently be easily given to him.

[25]   See pp.27-29 below for issues of eucharistic offering.

(iii) Ordained Ministers

Against this background, even with the tiny exceptions, Justin wavers not at all. Hebrews is constantly under contribution; Jesus Christ is our one high priest after the order of Melchisedek; and earthly ministers (save only 'the presider') are simply not there. Hebrews is, understandably, closer to hand in his debate with Trypho than in his address to the emperor, but echoes of it come in the *Apology*, as, e.g., where he calls Christ the 'apostle' in *Apol.*12 and 63 (cf. Heb.3.1), and the 'first-begotten' in *Apol.*63 (cf. Heb.1.6) – terms in the New Testament unique to Hebrews – and where he relies upon Psalm 2.7 and Psalm 110.1, which figure strongly in Hebrews.[26] In the *Dialogue* it is Psalm 110.4 and Christ as the high priest after the order of Melchisedek which constantly recur (see chs.19, 32-33, 34, 42, 63, 83, 86, 96, 113, 115, 118).[27]

So Justin avoids the linguistic risk in using the *hiereus* stem about Christian ministers. This is not, however, because he carefully chooses other terms – no, the way he avoids such risks is quite uncalculatingly simple: he virtually does not mention Christian ministers *at all*.[28] Bishops or presbyters do not occur. In *Apol.*61, the agents of baptism are simply the plural 'we' – with a passing mention of one 'who leads the candidate to the bath' and names the Trinity over him, but has no other characterization or visible appointment. In the eucharist Justin refers to *diakonoi* taking the bread and wine to those absent; and they might just be (in our terms) an ordained 'order' – or they might not.[29] There is necessary reference to the 'pre-sider' (*ho proestos*) at the eucharist (*Apol.*65,67) – and its connotation is indeterminate. The term is regularly translated as 'he who presides' or even 'the president', which would identify him chiefly by his function, not by his 'orders' or

---

[26] There are also echoes of Hebrews in individual words, as, e.g., in the deployment of the *photizo* stem to refer to conversion and baptism (see commentary on p.35 below), but this could have been simply part of the Christian linguistic currency, which, even if originally popularized by its use in Hebrews, does not of itself imply that Hebrews itself lay under Justin's gaze.

[27] There is an interesting juxtaposition of most of the quotations from the psalms found in Hebrews 1, along with the terminology of Christ as high priest, in 1 Clement 36, which might suggest a tradition of reference to Hebrews in Rome.

[28] A wonderful example of how a mind-set may affect a reading of patristic texts comes in the following: 'It may be conceded at once that neither Justin nor Irenaeus call Christian ministers "priests". But will anyone venture to claim that the line between ministers and laymen is in the least blurred by either of them?' (R.C.Moberley, *Ministerial Priesthood* (2ⁿᵈ ed, John Murray, London, 1907) p.86). But suppose there is no line, blurred or unblurred, between them in Justin *at all...*

[29] Some commentators also refer to a 'lector', as though there were an appointed office for reading the scriptures in the assembly. But *Apol.*67 only refers to 'the person reading' or 'the one who reads' in such informal language as to give no foothold for an office of 'reader' or 'lector'.

appointment in the ecclesial structure.[30] The presider was responsible for the distribution of the collection for the poor, and therefore held a pastoral role, but even so his function would be compatible with, say, that of officers appointed on an annually rotating basis![31] However, a case can obviously be made that *ho proestos* does imply a permanent office of authority, and thus means the (slightly veiled) 'bishop', but it is conjectural.[32] Justin promotes and defends a Christian faith in which the ordination and defined roles of ministers simply do not figure: 'orders' neither occupy the shop-window nor form some essential substructure. His aim is starkly to tell both Jew and emperor what Christians believe and what the assembly does, with minimal reference to organization.

So has Justin no earthly priests, no persons with cultic roles? He has, and he informs Trypho very clearly: 'we are the true high priestly race of God, as even God himself bears witness, saying that in every place among the Gentiles sacrifices are presented to him well-pleasing and pure. Now God receives sacrifices from no-one, except through his priests.' (*Dial.*116).[33] The identifying of the whole people of God as priestly and as offering spiritual sacrifices echoes 1 Peter 2.5 and 2.9 (and the background in Exod.19). So Justin, while deploying his argument against Trypho, quite

---

[30] Ignatius' famously wrote 'Let that be held a valid [*or* secure *or* trustworthy] eucharist which is under the bishop or *one to whom he shall have committed it*' (*Smyrn.*8 – my italics). This is distant in time and space and ethos from Justin, but it might just possibly be a general second century principle, and, if so, might suggest that for Justin, even if a bishop might sometimes be *ho proestos*, he did not always have to be, and at other times someone else was chartered by him to preside, and issues of 'orders' were not near the forefront of the decision-taking. But in any case Peter Lampe demonstrates a far more strongly self-sufficient and self-perpetuating form to local assemblies (see, P.Lampe, *From Paul to Valentinus,op.cit.* pp.374-377 and elsewhere), and no bishop is part of it.

[31] To put it most starkly, an advocate of an 'Independent' or 'Congregationalist' church polity would find good precedent in Justin, and nothing contrary to it at all.

[32] This is discussed by Trevor Jalland in 'Justin Martyr and the President of the Eucharist' in *Studia Patristica 5* (1962) pp.83-85. He shows some instances in classical, biblical and early Christian literature where *ho proestos* seems to denote the holder of a permanent office. However, not only was Jalland (from his own anglo-catholicism) pressing a case in order to find and establish the presence and role of a bishop in Justin's account, but he himself admits an 'ambiguity in the language of the New Testament' (see Rom.12.8; 1 Thess.5.12; 1 Tim.5.17; Tit.3.8). Interestingly, the verb is used in a contingent adjectival way, rather than as a verbal noun, in Hermas *Shepherd* Vis.2.iv, 'the elders who preside'. Jalland's conclusion that translators should render *ho proestos ton adelphon* as 'he who rules over the brethren' has been largely ignored since, as inspection of translations will reveal.

[33] The transition from specially appointed Old Testament priests to the understanding that Christian believers as a whole are priests is reinforced by Justin's argument leading to this conclusion in *Dial.*116 – for he uses Joshua the high priest being stripped of filthy garments to equip him for his priestly ministry (Zech.3.3-9) as the paradigm for us all being stripped of our sins by Christ to become the 'true high priestly race of God'.

unselfconsciously locates himself here in clear conformity to both Hebrews and 1 Peter.[34]

(iv) The First Day of the Week

In *Dial.* 41 Justin cites 'the first day after the Sabbath' (an obvious term for his Jewish audience) as the day on which Jesus rose from the dead, though without including any special observance of the day.[35] In *Apol.*67 he says the assembly takes place on the day that is called 'Sun-day', which seems to be the first extant use by a Christian author of the Roman nomenclature for dating the first day of the week. There can be no doubt that this *is* the first day of the week, and conforms to 'first day' in the Scriptures (*mia sabbaton*), and the 'Lord's day' (*kuriake*) in Rev.1.6, *Didache* 14.1 and Ignatius *Magnesians* 9.1. It is highly probable that this is also the 'stato die' to which Pliny refers, as reported to him by the erstwhile Christians whom he had tortured, as the occasion on which they had (25 years earlier) regularly met. Justin undoubtedly means the first day of the Jewish week, but at this stage he helpfully identifies the day to the emperor by its name within the Roman week.[36] At the end of the chapter he then relates the two calendars to each other, insisting that Sun-day is the first day of the week (fixed as such by God's beginning the creation on that day), and it qualifies as the proper day for the Christian assembly as the day that Jesus Christ rose from the dead. As noted, he also emphasizes the day of the resurrection in *Dial.* 41, where he calls it the 'eighth day'. 'Eighth day' has a 'mystical meaning' in *Dial.*24, and it recurs in *Dial.*138, where, arguing somewhat improbably from the eight persons of Noah's family saved from the deluge, Justin again uses this slightly oblique term for the day of Christ's resurrection (again without connecting

---

[34]   It is worth noting that, in the whole of the two documents, Justin uses the word 'church' (*ekklesia*) only twice (in *Dial.*63 and 134, the latter use in a characteristically far-fetched assertion of typology that 'Leah is your people and synagogue; but Rachel is our church'), and he employs the corporate concept of an ecclesial entity little more – the phrase 'true high priestly race of God' (see footnote 33 opposite) being one of those rare occasions (and Christians as a new 'race' (*genos*) recurs in *Dial.* 135 and 138). Justin's 'apologias' to both Jew and emperor concentrate almost entirely on the person of Christ as being the Son of God who fulfils the prophecies, and believers in him are simply called 'Christians'. So there is little ecclesial context within which issues of 'orders' might have emerged. Even the description of baptisms in *Apol.*61, while it gives a strong suggestion of 'incorporation' in the procedures followed, prefers actual wording of an individualistic sort (see E(iii) on pp.17-18 below). Justin's insistence in *Apol.*66 that only the baptized can participate in communion does more to convey incorporation than any baptismal language used itself.

[35]   See the text on pp. 35 and 45 below.

[36]   W.Rordorf calls this the 'planetary week' – i.e. a week of seven days (which easily therefore coalesces with the Christian week derived from the Jewish revelation), with the days named after the planets. Sun-day appears to have been the second day in this week. The week's origins lie in the dawn of the Roman Empire. See W.Rordorf, *Sunday* (ET, SCM, 1968) pp.24-38.

it with any assembly for worship).[37] The identifying of this day is of course in line with Ignatius' commendation of the Lord's Day to the Magnesians, not only as distinguishing them from keeping sabbaths, but also as commemorating the rising of Christ from the dead.[38]

It would be fruitless to seek a liturgical year in Justin's works. While the keeping of the first day of the week in commemoration of the resurrection is the background to the Quartodeciman controversy about when to observe the Christian *Pasch*, the controversy itself was only just breaking ground at the time when Justin wrote the *Apology*.[39] Neither the baptismal rite in *Apol*.61 nor any of the eucharistic evidence gives us any hint of an annual cycle of observances.[40]

E. Baptism
(i) Compared with circumcision
Baptism has close parallels to circumcision, both being once-for-all-for-life initiatory ceremonies. In the scriptures circumcision is related to the covenant promises of God to Abraham (Gen.17), and is expounded by Paul as 'the sign of circumcision, a seal of the righteousness which he [Abraham] had by faith when he was still uncircumcised' (Rom.4.11), an exposition not far distant from Paul's own understanding of baptism (as, e.g., in Rom.6.3-4). True circumcision is of the heart (Deut. 30.6; Jer.9.25-26), not the sign 'made with hands' (cf. Col. 2.11-12), and this significance is not only regularly picked up by Justin, but is reported by him as the inner part of baptism also - as 'we...have received not carnal but spiritual circumcision...And we have received it through baptism...' (*Dial*.43.2). Justin has a series of links between circumcision as a type and its baptismal fulfilment, and they may be portrayed thus:

---

[37]   A further instance of 'the eighth day' comes in *Ep.Barnabas* 15.9, for the author expounds it as the day on which Christians commemorate Christ's resurrection from the dead. Marginally less obvious, and yet unmistakable in its significance for the first day of the week, is Jesus' appearing to (doubting) Thomas 'after eight days' (John 20.26).

[38]   Justin himself never attempts any continuity from sabbath to 'first day' – the sabbath is fulfilled by the whole of life being a rest in Christ (see *Dial*.12); and the first day echoes creation and commemorates the resurrection.

[39]   If Polycarp's visit to Anicetus to discuss the appropriate day for the Pasch (Eusebius, *HE*. IV.14.1) is to be dated in the 150s (see footnote 7 above), then Justin perhaps wrote in the very last days before the issue surfaced in Rome – or at least was distant from the controversy.

[40]   'Justin Martyr...carefully described the rites of initiation as distinct from the regular Sunday assembly. He does not assign that initiatory rite to a particular time in the year, however, nor does he suggest that it occurs only once in the year.' (Thomas J.Talley, *The Origins of the Liturgical Year* (Pueblo, New York, 1986) p.37)

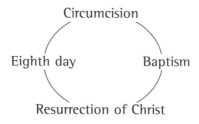

Circumcision

Eighth day   Baptism

Resurrection of Christ

The passages below (see pages 33-35) which relate baptism to circumcision exhibit various elements in this linkage, though not necessarily all four items in any one passage.

(ii) Ritual
The description of the actual baptism in *Apol*.61 is actually very light on what we would call liturgical detail. The candidates have been instructed, have fasted in preparation, and have committed themselves to Christian discipleship. They are taken to water, in a place of baptism away from the worshipping assembly. There there is 'named' over them the Father, the Son and the Holy Spirit, but we do not know the mode of baptism, nor the formula, if any, in which the naming occurred. No particular officiant is mentioned – as stated, the 'washing' is performed by a plural 'us'. How many persons accompanied the candidate (Justin changes to the singular), or what their respective functions were, we cannot tell, save only that one person 'leads the candidate to the water' and 'names the name' over him. And the only further action described is the bringing of him into the assembly to join in the prayers, the kiss [41] and the communion.

(iii) Metaphors
An earlier discussion (see page 15 note 34 above) pointed out that although the character of the baptismal rite in *Apol*.61 demonstrated 'incorporation', the terminology used looked relatively individualistic. The terms to express the significance of the rite are nevertheless well rooted in the New Testament, chief among them being 'washing' (*Apol*. 61,65, 66; cf. Acts 22.16, 1 Cor.6.11, Titus 3.5[42]), 'enlightenment' (*Dial*.39,122; cf. Eph.1.18, Heb.6.4), 'being made disciples' (*Apol*.15, *Dial*.39; cf. Matt.28.19, Acts 14.21) and 'rebirth' (*Dial*.138; *Apol*.61,65; cf.John 3.3, Titus 3.5, 1 Peter 1.23). Possibly the use of Noah and his ark as a type suggests belonging to a saved community (*Dial*.138; cf. 1 Peter 3.18-22, 2 Peter 2.5).

[41]   This defers the question as to whether the kiss was itself initiatory, which is discussed on pp.21 and 48 below.
[42]   The *louo* stem provides the words translated as both 'washing' and 'bath' in English.

But other Old Testament typology Justin cites – such as Elisha making the axe float (*Dial.*86.6; cf 2 Kings 6. 5-7) [43] - is like his selected New Testament imagery in not particularly identifying communal significance. Justin has a church in practice, but without much overt ecclesiology.[44]

(iv) Infants?

Justin's accounts of baptism nowhere mention candidates too young to answer for themselves, which in broad terms is also the case in the New Testament, in Ignatius and *Didache*, and also in the description of actual baptisms in Tertullian's *De Baptismo*. However, Tertullian tells us elsewhere that infants were being baptized. Hippolytus' liturgical pattern is similarly silent about infant candidates, but the opening 'rubrics' tell us that they are at times present. Indeed there is good reason to think infants were baptized with their families from the start[45]; so did Justin know nothing of such candidates or, alternatively, does he take them totally for granted, as not needing to be identified among the candidates? There is one slightly recondite point where Justin has been called in evidence on behalf of pedobaptism, and hence the passage from *Apol.*15 below, and the commentary on it and on the associated *Dial.*39.

(v) Confirmation?

From 1890 to 1970 Anglican authors generally took almost as axiomatic an 'integrated' original initiation rite, composed of water-baptism plus confirmation (by laying on of hands or anointing), leading into communion. This required an over-focussing on two passages in Acts (8.14-17; 19.1-6) at the expense of both the other seven references to baptisms in Acts and all the references in the Pauline Epistles.[46] But, because this 'two-stage initiation' doctrine has to assert an invariable practice from the apostles onwards, any post-apostolic writer on baptism who shows no knowledge of 'confirmation' presents a problem – and Justin is the *locus classicus* of the problem, as he gives no hint of such a post-baptismal ceremony. So the argument has had either to leave Justin out of the account, or somehow to portray him as telling a different story

---

[43]   The location of this miracle at the Jordan seems to have been influential in motivating Justin (and others after him) to see in it a type of baptism.

[44]   See p.15 note 34 above.

[45]   I press this strongly in my *A Case for Infant Baptism* (Grove Booklet on Ministry and Worship no.20, 1973) and *Infant Baptism and the Gospel* (DLT, 1993) pp.14-33.

[46]   For an answer to these generations teaching a 'two-stage' sacramental initiation, see: G.W.H.Lampe, *The Seal of the Spirit* (Longmans, 1951); J.D.G.Dunn, *Baptism in the Holy Spirit* (SCM, 1970); E.C.Whitaker, *Sacramental Initiation Complete in Baptism* (Grove Liturgical Study no.1, 1975); COB, *Anglican Confirmation* (Grove Liturgical Study no.48, 1986); David Holeton (ed), *Growing in Newness of Life: Christian Initiation in Anglicanism Today* (ABC, Toronto, 1993).

from what appears on the surface of his text.[47] The argument has called in aid passages from *Dial.*87 and 88, and so they are duly provided below, and the argument is then confronted in the commentary. But if Justin had no such ceremony, no hypothesis of an unbroken tradition from the apostles can survive.

F. Eucharist
(i) Overall pattern
Justin states in *Apol.*67 that the normal Sunday eucharist matches the baptismal eucharist in *Apol.*65. The resemblance is best seen by a simple comparative table:

Apol.65 Baptismal Eucharist	Apol.67 Sunday Eucharist
[Baptism outside the assembly and bringing in of newly baptized]	
1.	Readings
2.	Exhortation by President
3. Prayers by assembly	Prayers by assembly
4. Kiss of peace	
5. Bringing in of bread and wine	Bringing in of bread and wine
6. Thanksgivings offered by President	Thanksgivings offered by President
7. 'Amen' by assembly	'Amen' by assembly
8. Distribution to the assembly	Distribution to the assembly
9. Taking of elements to the absent by the deacons	Taking of elements to the absent by the deacons
10.	Collection of money and substance for the needy

It is very easy to turn these closely matching accounts into a common 'shape' thus:

      1-2.   Ministry of the word
         3.   The prayers
      4-8.   The eucharistic meal
    9-10. After communion

[47] It is inadequate for those who affirm the 'two-stage' initiation as *the* apostolic pattern to find evidence of a post-baptismal ceremony in nooks or crannies of the second century, for they need to demonstrate a use *as universal as water-baptism.* Thus, while J.D.C.Fisher attempted to find a continuity of initiatory anointing in Tertullian's references to Marcion's practice, even if successful, he would only have demonstrated one instance of usage, not a universal practice (and in *Anglican Confirmation (op.cit.*p.14) I have shown how very doubtful Fisher's case is – clearly a scholarship of despair in the face of both Justin's silence, and, presumably, the self-evident inadequacy of the Ratcliff argument on p.36 below).

The baptismal eucharist not only in principle followed a 'normal' Sunday practice, but Justin, having described it first, then refers back to it ('as I mentioned just now') in order to convey the nature of the normal Sunday celebration without repeating in *Apol.* 67 every detail already given in *Apol.* 65. We then have two alternative possibilities as to how the baptismal eucharist itself began: clearly the assembly as a whole is not attending the baptism, but 'the brothers are gathered together' in their place of assembly, and the newly baptized person is brought to them. They may have begun with a standard 'ministry of the word' (presumably with readings from scripture, and perhaps a sermon), or have waited in silence or used some other, perhaps baptismally focussed, form of prayer, praise, hymnody or meditative expectation. We are left to speculate.

(ii) Readings

Justin's account of the Sunday eucharist in *Apol.*67 begins with the reading of 'the memoirs (*apomnemoneumata*) of the apostles or the writings (*suggrammata*) of the prophets.' He regularly refers elsewhere to the 'memoirs of the apostles' (cf. *Dial.*103,105,106), and in *Apol.*66 he adds, when citing the 'memoirs', the relative clause 'which are called "gospels"' The writings of the 'prophets' clearly comprehend the whole Old Testament (for the books we call 'historical', not least the 'Books of Moses', are regularly called 'prophetic' by Justin, as well as the major and minor prophets). We seem therefore to have a twofold concept of what is now called scripture: the Old Testament and the Gospels. These are not only the two categories of what is read at the Sunday eucharist – they are also the two categories from which Justin constantly quotes. So full are his quotes from these two sources in both the *Dialogue* and the *Apology* that the lack of mention of Paul is intriguing.[48] Yet, even if Paul is not overtly mentioned, Justin's discussion of circumcision (as, e.g. in the *Dialogue* passages in (b)(i) below) gives a strong sense of his knowing the Pauline arguments. His knowledge of Hebrews and 1 Peter has been scrutinized earlier.[49] Those things said, the reading of an 'epistle' at the eucharist cannot be attested;

[48] So apparently lacking is any direct reference by Justin to Paul, that, despite scattered allusions, Robert Daly asserted that Justin was ignorant of Paul's letters (*The Origins of the Christian Doctrine of Sacrifice* (Fortress/DLT, 1978) pp.88-89). But of all the places where Paul's letters could be unknown in the mid-second century, surely Rome was the most unlikely? Paul had written weightily to the Romans; he had been in Rome at least once; he had written up to seven letters from there; his 1 Corinthians is cited at length in 1 Clem. 47, from Rome; Ignatius of Antioch clearly knew a Pauline corpus (cf. his *Ephesians* 12.2) and Paul and his writings are clearly in view in his *Romans* (a letter kept carefully?); and Marcion accepted ten letters of Paul and discarded three. The concept of 'canon' is usually attributed to the conflict with Marcion, whereas previously the only question would have been what was actually read in the assembly on Sundays (where Justin himself is a key, if vague, witness).

[49] See pp.13-15 above.

we have to read Justin simply as he is. That itself sets us problems, as in *Apol.*67 he has Gospels before Old Testament, he probably has them as alternatives to each other, and they are read 'as long as time allows', which looks like a pre-lectionary situation. The presider's address follows, and is stated to expound and apply what the scriptures have taught.

(iii) Prayers and the Kiss

The manner of the prayers appears to have been highly congregational, and the first person plural description of what 'we' do in the prayers contrasts in both accounts with the third person singular ('he') of the later presidential thanksgiving over the bread and cup. So, if here 'we' are 'making prayers', was it a free-for-all? Some known or designated pray-ers may be implied, but it reads more easily as though any who wished articulated prayers and thanksgivings as he (or she?) saw fit. If so, Justin's account is not far distant from 1 Cor.14, though rarely matched in later patristic developments.

The kiss is only mentioned in the baptismal account, which *could* possibly suggest it was unique to baptisms (and perhaps itself initiatory?) rather than a normal Sunday use. But, as Justin, having described the prayers in the baptismal rite, then alludes to them much more briefly in the Sunday one ('as I mentioned just now'), so, in the same way he may well have simply not bothered to mention the kiss a second time.[50] If the kiss was used each Sunday, then its role looks like that of a lead-in to sharing the meal – by it worshippers identified themselves as Christians and reaffirmed their mutual love on the threshold of the sacred meal.[51]

(iv) Preparation of the Elements

Both accounts have a 'bringing in' of bread and a cup of mixed water and wine at this point, introducing the second half of the rite, often today called the 'liturgy of the sacrament'. Gregory Dix classified this as the first action of a 'four-action shape', the uniting of two originally separate dominical acts, i.e. the 'taking' by Jesus of first the bread and, 'after supper', the cup.[52] As there is now no larger meal context, the two elements are provided together – but the wholly natural 'laying of the table' is no more than preparatory (like Jesus' disciples going ahead to get the passover room ready), and provides no hint of Dix's developed

---

[50] The possibility of the kiss being initiatory is discussed further in the commentary on p.48 below.
[51] This seems the likely rationale. However, Tertullian's famous 'signaculum orationis' ('the seal of prayer' – and the mutual acceptance of those praying together, Tert. *De Orat.* 18) should not be dismissed, but may not bear upon understandings in Justin's time.
[52] See Dix, *The Shape of the Liturgy* (Dacre, 1945) pp.111f.

'offertory theology'.[53] The elements are apparently placed before the president, and in the baptismal eucharist we read that he 'takes' them (or possibly 'receives' them) before beginning the thanksgiving. This is clearly distinguished from the 'bringing in' which is already complete, and, while the 'taking' identified the elements (and constituted the first of the 'dominical' acts), it is devoid of any doctrinal significance.

There is an oddity in the phrase 'water and wine mixed with water' in *Apol.*65. The idea that 'wine mixed with water' (*kramatos*) is a clumsy, redundant scribal addition is backed by some manuscript evidence, examined in a footnote below. Furthermore, in *Dial.*70 Justin, quoting Isaiah 33 'Bread shall be given to him, and his water shall be sure' (see page 45 below), says this is prophesying the bread and cup which Christ commanded to his disciples. This citation, it is urged, suggests it was a contemporary practice of bread and water in the eucharist which led Justin to the prophecy in Isaiah.[54] Biblical and patristic writers are usually reckoned to imply wine as the eucharistic drink, even when saying simply 'the cup'.[55] That does not fully determine the use of wine in Justin's

[53] See COB, *The End of the Offertory* (Grove Liturgical Study 14, Nottingham, 1978) pp.7-8. Whatever later authors may suggest in terms of ceremonializing the bringing in or preparing of the elements, Justin gives no support to it. The stark verdict of Joseph Jungmann is 'The faithful themselves do not bring the gifts...Nor is any offertory procession yet in vogue.' (*The Early Liturgy*, DLT edn, London, 1960, p.41). Robert Taft says the action is 'so simple that it cannot even be called a ritual' (*The Great Entrance*, Orientalia Christiana Analecta 200, 2nd ed. Rome, 1978, p.12). M.B.Moreton, with a vested interest in patristic precedents, wrote on 'Offertory Processions' in *Studia Patristica* XVII (Pt 2, 1982) pp.569-570, but only began the discussion with Tertullian, without any mention of Justin.

[54] The hypothesis began with A.Harnack in the 1880s, but was dubbed 'more ingenious than convincing' by A.W.F.Blunt in *The Apologies of Justin Martyr* (Cambridge, 1911) p.xliv. It was more recently revived by Andrew McGowan in his *Ascetic Eucharists: Food and Drink in Early Christian Ritual Meals* (Clarendon Press, Oxford, 1999) pp.151-4. Bradshaw airs it not unsympathetically in *Eucharistic Origins*, pp.76-77. But it requires that Codex Bobbonianus (incorrectly called 'Bobbianus' by recent authors, perhaps from a misprint in L.W.Barnard in 1967), which omits '*kai kramatos*', is independent of the Parisian manuscript and superior to it, and that later scribes have inserted into the Parisian text not only *kai kramatos*, but also *oinos* later in chs.65 and 67. If Bobbonianus is simply a poor, even careless, copy of the Parisian text, then its omissions are of no consequence and Justin's references to wine must stand – and his comparisons to events with water (the somewhat far-fetched interpretation of Is.33 in *Dial.*70 and the allegation of Mithraic imitation in *Apol.*66) then rely on a more general 'food and drink' resemblance (note Justin's own inclusive 'solid and liquid food' in *Dial.*117) rather than a specific 'bread and water' phenomenon. These passages quoted for comparison could equally be matched and reversed by *Dial.*54, where Justin quotes Gen.49.11, and, without mentioning the eucharist, almost equates wine (the 'blood of the grape'!) with the blood of Christ.

[55] 'Cup' is the usual New Testament term, whereby the communicant drinks of Christ's blood (Matt.26.27; Mk.14.23; 1 Cor.10.16; 11.25, 26, 28), and the inference that at the Last Supper the cup contained wine originates in 'I will no more drink of the fruit of the vine until I drink it new in my Father's kingdom'. *Oinos* itself occurs in no New Testament eucharistic contexts! *Didache* again has the 'cup', though the thanksgiving gives thanks for the 'holy vine of David', a curiously juxtaposed phrase if the cup did *not* contain wine. Ignatius speaks of the eucharistic 'bread' – and of Christ's flesh and blood – but without mentioning cup or wine. After Justin's time Irenaeus associates bread and cup with Christ's flesh and blood, also without identifying the element within the cup. Justin alone mentions what is brought into the celebration, and alone mentions *oinos*, and thus the presence of *oinos* in *Apol.*65 and 67 is more significant than its absence elsewhere.

account, if (which is under question) there is no direct evidence for it, but it perhaps loads the probabilities towards wine.

Mixed water and wine should not be seen through latterday eyes as carrying symbolism. The 'mixing' occurred outside of the assembly, not ritually. There is reason to think wine drunk in this period was well diluted in any case[56]; and thus the term *krama* may well imply a usual commodity rather than special provision – and be interchangeable with *oinos*. If Justin had any particular purpose in mentioning its composition, it was probably to deflect any idea that the emperor might have gleaned that the eucharist was an occasion of drunkenness.

(v) Eucharistic Prayer(s)

From the congregational prayers (see (iii) above) we come to the presidential thanksgiving – articulated by him alone once the elements are on the table, but endorsed at the end by the congregation's 'amen'. In the baptismal eucharist he prays 'at considerable length'; in the Sunday one 'according to his ability'. Both imply that he has freedom in composing his prayer, and that 'thanksgiving' is the central theme of the praying – it is a 'eucharistic prayer'. However, both also include 'prayers' in the plural alongside 'thanksgiving', which has led Bradshaw cautiously to support a theory of two separate thanksgivings uttered over the two elements separately.[57] This looks unlikely, for the two elements are first brought in together, are then 'taken' together by the president, and are afterwards distributed together. Furthermore, the terminology used in *Apol*.66 to denote the prayer which 'eucharisticizes' the elements, determining their 'transformation' is 'the word of prayer which comes from him'. This reads grammatically as a single prayer – and the single 'amen' reported in both accounts surely also indicates a single prayer, and confirms that conclusion?

If this is so, then the plural term 'prayers' simply indicates the variegated contents of the 'eucharistic prayer'. We can discern a sufficiently common pattern for Justin to say that the president praises the Father through the

---

[56]   Cf Acts 2.15, where the implication is, presumably, that even excessive drinking would not get one drunk by 9 a.m.!

[57]   *Eucharistic Origins*, pp.75-76. Bradshaw quotes Enrico Mazza, *The Origins of the Eucharistic Prayer* (ET by Ronald E.Lane, Liturgical Press, Collegeville, 1995) p.60, but Mazza is focussed far more upon *Didache* and his brief mention of Justin is not closely argued, and ignores the contrary points summarized above. Bradshaw, following Mazza, also adduces later evidence in *Didascalia* to support this theory (*Eucharistic Origins*, pp.104-5 and 122), but it is unclear that that evidence actually points that way, and Mazza's connecting *Didache* to this later Syrian document looks rather like 'lumping'.

Son and the Holy Spirit and thanks God 'that we have been counted worthy of these things from him'. The very mention of 'these things' implies that the thanksgiving referred in some way to the elements, though it could simply refer to the nature and saving acts of God. The explanation in *Apol*.66 suggests strongly that it included a petition for the 'transformation' of the elements, and possibly also a petition for the transformation of the communicants through receiving them. If the first part of any eucharistic prayer involved trinitarian praise of God, and the second half focussed the needs and privileges of the assembly, along with Christ's 'nourishment' (*Apol*.66) of them, there was a discernible outline shape and a given complex content to a genuinely extemporary prayer.

In *Apol*.66 Justin declares that the elements are, by this prayer, 'eucharisticized' into Christ's very flesh and blood. Once the words of Christ in institution are taken seriously (and they are, of course, cited there), then there is inevitably a 'before' (when they are bread and wine) and an 'after' (when they are his flesh and blood). Thus a 'transformation' logically links them – a doctrine of 'consecration' is developing. For our purposes, we now distinguish between what effects consecration (ie, the 'eucharisticizing' prayer), and what consecration effects (ie, that, in some sense, the elements become Christ's flesh and blood).[58] The latter question is examined in section (vii) below.

In *Apol*.66, the eucharisticization is described as effected 'through the word of prayer which comes from him' (*'di' euches logou tou par' autou'*). This must mean the eucharistic prayer, but it has been variously expounded by scholars. John McKenna identifies five possible interpretations:
1. A prayer *for* the Logos – i.e. a kind of epiclesis (capital 'L' is editorial but true to much of Justin);
2. A prayer *from* the (personal) Logos (with the capital 'L' again);
3. A prayer of words (stemming) from him (Christ) – ie the institution narrative;
4. The word of prayer (coming) from him (Christ) – i.e. a whole eucharistic prayer including the institution narrative;
5. A general sort of prayer.[59]

---

[58] This distinction is vital to all analyses of historic eucharistic liturgy and doctrine, as no one theory of 'what effects consecration' - the liturgical question - necessarily entails any one outcome as to 'what consecration effects' – the doctrinal question (see my *Eucharistic Consecration*, Grove Worship Series 148, 1998).

[59] John H. McKenna, *Eucharist and Holy Spirit* (Alcuin/Mayhew-McCrimmon, 1975) pp.50-51.

McKenna himself discounts nos. 2 and 5 of these, but says of the other three 'It is difficult to come up with a clear-cut judgment'. We may, however, trace a slowly developing historical debate about it.

In 1980 Geoffrey Cuming, drawing a careful parallel with phrasing in *Apol.*13, proposed 'through a prayer of the form of words that is from him', meaning the institution narrative (McKenna's no.3), which Justin quotes in the next sentence.[60] Anthony Gelston replied, saying that the institution narrative cannot be called 'a prayer', and Justin's discussion explains 'eucharisticized' as a prayer of thanksgiving offered 'in conformity with the pattern of Jesus' thanksgiving at the Last Supper' (no.4).[61] A key element for him is in the Sunday account, 'offers up prayers and thanksgiving, according to his ability', which implies an extemporary, or at most personally prepared, form of words, and excludes a given formula. However, an interesting attempt to bring no.1 into play came more recently from Michael Heintz – the key being to read *logos* as 'the Word' (with a capital), and *par' autou* as 'from him (ie God)'.[62] The upshot is then that 'this enigmatic phrase...reflects not an institution narrative, but a theology of eucharistic consecration which is consistent with the development of an epiclesis of the *logos*'.[63]

The actual content of the prayer may not be materially affected by whether Gelston or Heintz wins the prize. The evidence points to an extemporary but weighty ('*epi polu'*) thanksgiving, with an overall Trinitarian shape, in which the Father is addressed through the Son, and the works of God in creation and redemption are no doubt strongly in view. The participants are themselves also the theme of thanksgiving, having been 'counted worthy of these things' – and we can visualize petitions for them to fit naturally in the latter part of the prayer. There might be no standardized narrative of institution, but extemporary reference to how the Lord had commanded his disciples to commemorate him would no doubt often, if not always, occur.

(vi) Narrative of Institution
Justin is the first extant post-apostolic author to quote Jesus' words of institution. While the account in *Apol.* 66 is close to scripture and not unlike the simple narrative found in later rites, Justin is quoting it neither for its dominical charter to observe the Supper, nor for its interpretation of

[60] *JTS* 31 (1980) pp.80-82.
[61] *JTS* 33 (1982) pp.173-175.
[62] There is an intriguing precedent in Luke 6.12, where *proseuche tou Theou* (literally 'prayer of God') must mean 'prayer to God'.
[63] *Studia Liturgica* 33 (2003) pp.37-61.

the bread and cup. *Apol.* 66, following Justin's first account of the eucharist, is written to assure the emperor that only baptized Christians gather for the eucharist. The crucial words in the sentence containing the narrative are not 'this is my body' and 'this is my blood' but the last words of all: 'and he shared it with them alone'. This distances us from our own question as to how the narrative came to his mind – a question whether it featured in the extempore eucharistic prayers, or whether, without being quoted in the rite, it was used *verbatim* in catechetical or more informal contexts?[64] Perhaps Justin even quotes a narrative rarely heard aloud in either worship or catechesis, but simply draws upon his undoubted knowledge of the Gospels to inform the emperor.[65] A weekly eucharist, known as dominical in origin, might well be continuing by its momentum, without being constantly 'fuelled' by recitation of the verbal narrative, internally in the liturgical rite, or externally in catechesis.

Even an hypothesis that the narrative *was* regularly quoted in the eucharistic prayer does not identify its recitation with a 'moment' of consecration – which much of the later Western church has assumed. It might have been either or both of an historical warrant for the eucharist and an authoritative interpretation of it, and yet not be 'consecratory'. Justin locates 'consecration' in 'eucharisticization', of which the narrative, if it were in use, may have been part but can hardly have been the major content. As the thanksgiving was extempore, Jesus' institution may have been cited on some occasions, and not on others, or briefly on some occasions and more fully on others.

(vii) Transformation of the Elements
So what does Justin teach about what consecration effects? He frankly tells an emperor who may imprison him or worse that this is the 'flesh' (*sarx*) of Jesus by a 'conversion' or 'transformation' process, comparable both to the incarnation and to the physical nourishment which transforms our physical selves. There are no ifs and buts – the language is as 'realist'

---

[64] Ratcliff, without insisting that 'the word of prayer which comes from him' *is* the narrative, yet located the narrative firmly within the eucharistic prayer in at least the baptismal eucharist, and added 'From occasional to regular use is but a short step' (in 'The Eucharistic Institution Narrative of Justin Martyr's *First Apology*', reprinted from *JEH* April 1971 in A.H.Couratin and D.H.Tripp (edd), *E.C.Ratcliff: Liturgical Studies* (SPCK, 1976) p.44). John Austin Baker, opining that the narrative was catechetical in 1 Corinthians, nevertheless thinks 'Justin...shows that in his day the words of institution had become part of the thanksgiving over the bread and wine' (in 'The "Institution" Narratives and the Christian Eucharist' in Church of England Doctrine Commission, *Thinking about the Eucharist* (SCM, 1972) pp.54-55) – but does Justin 'show' that?

[65] His actual words look Pauline (or from the longer text of Luke?), but, as he reverses the order of 'This is my body' and 'Do this...', and changes 'my remembrance' (*ten emen anamnesin*) into 'remembrance of me' (*ten anamnesin mou*), he is probably giving general expression to the tradition, rather than quoting *verbatim*.

as Jesus' words; indeed *sarx* echoes John 6 rather than the Synoptics (despite the actual quotation 'This is my body'). As we know nothing of any first or second century debates about how this transformation was understood, we can hardly allocate it to one or other of post-Reformation categories.[66] Thus, while Eric Mascall can quote *Apol.*66 to show 'how extremely realistic and unmetaphorical the doctrine of the early fathers on the eucharistic presence is'[67], Cranmer himself can quote the end of *Apol.*65 to show that what the deacons take to the absent is 'bread and wine and water'.[68] An interesting reflection comes from Robert Taft, quoting from J.C.McGowan:

> 'These customs [i.e., the cultus of reserved elements] reveal... that the eucharist was revered [in early centuries] more as a thing than as a person. Great reverence was paid to this sacred thing, this Body of the Lord...but still...more a respect for a holy object than recognition of a divine person to be adored.'

Taft adds:

> 'But by the turn of the fourth and fifth century we already see the beginnings of a significant shift in eucharistic consciousness.'[69]

Justin comes well before that 'significant shift' – but in fact says nothing about revering the elements. The point about them being Christ's flesh and blood is simply that, being consumed, they should transform us. The three major eucharistic passages in the *Dialogue* simply speak artlessly of the bread and the cup, certainly as commemorating Christ's suffering, but without mention of actual 'flesh' or 'blood'. And in the *Apology* itself the deacons only take 'eucharisticized bread and wine and water' to the absent. So Justin's understanding is left undetermined.

(viii) Eucharistic Sacrifice

It is notorious that Justin states in *Dial.*41 and 117 that the eucharist – and perhaps the very bread and cup of the eucharist – is a sacrifice.[70] Both contexts are ones where Justin asserts an Old Testament eucharistic connection, in *Dial.*41 to demonstrate an analogy with one kind of Old Testament sacrifice (the response of the cleansed leper), and in both

---

66 While *Didache* does not relate the bread and wine to the flesh and blood of Christ at all, Ignatius does so in 'realist' terms, when he illustrates the Gnostics' denial of the incarnation by saying 'they do not confess that the eucharist is the flesh of our Saviour Jesus Christ' (*Smyrn.*6).

67 E.L.Mascall, *Corpus Christi* (2nd ed, Longmans, 1965) p.72.

68 *On the Lord's Supper*, pp.263-4.

69 Robert F.Taft in 'Is there Devotion to the Holy Eucharist in the Christian East?' in *Worship* Vol.80 No.3 (May 2006) p.218 – quoting J.C.McGowan, *Concelebration: Sign of the Unity of the Church* (New York, 1964) pp.13-15

70 The 'perhaps' in my parenthesis derives not only from Justin's following point, that only Christian lives constitute our sacrifice, but also from the subtle distinction between Justin's two expositions. In *Dial.*41 he states directly that the bread and cup *are* our sacrifices: but in *Dial.*117 our sacrifices are offered *in* or *at* 'the eucharist of the bread and cup', which is wholly compatible with his following point that holy lives are our only sacrifices.

chapters to assert from Mal.1.11-12 that the eucharist fulfils a prophecy which contrasted a pure sacrifice of a promised new Gentile dispensation with the inadequate ones of the old dispensation of Malachi's time. The passage is quoted in *Didache* 14 as well as four times in Justin. However, Justin's first use of it (*Dial*.28-29) makes no explicit connection with the eucharist, which may provide a clue about its role in early Christian literature. Clearly, at a very early point the Malachi passage helped Christians to distinguish themselves from Jews, and to demonstrate God's favour towards them in place of the Jews. This is almost certainly in view in the *Didache*[71], and could hardly be more forcefully exemplified than in Justin's fourfold quotation of it to convert Trypho. The Malachi passage may not have been in universal Christian currency, but these two greatly disparate early uses do suggest a widespread reliance upon it to promote the Christian dispensation above the Jewish one *from the Jewish scriptures*. As scripture, once in regular use it was unlikely to be reviewed or abandoned – yet the New Testament writers had not used it, and the teaching of Hebrews, in the light of the once-for-all sacrifice of Christ on the cross, excluded ritual sacrifice from Christian assemblies.

On this analysis, as Mal.1.11 became a proof text over against the Jews, so the eucharist, fulfilling the prophecy, was at intervals described as in some unexplored sense 'a sacrifice'. However, that unhelpful adoption of sacrificial terminology has in Justin to be tempered by some qualifying considerations:

(i)   None of his four citations of Mal.1.11 relates the 'sacrifice' to the obtaining of some benefit;

(ii)   None of them in any way suggests that we offer Christ himself or his sacrifice to the Father;

(iii)   In *Dial*.117 the statement that we offer the sacrifice to God in or at the eucharist is followed immediately by the explanatory statement that holy lives are the only sacrifice we can offer;

(iv)   No language of a sacrifice we offer occurs in the accounts of eucharistic practice in *Apol*.65 and 67 – the theme is thanksgiving – or in *Apol*.66, where the theme is about how the elements change and change us.

(v)   Whatever sacrifices we offer, *we* are corporately the priests who offer them – Christians have no class of distinctive 'priests' with a ritual role to offer the bread and cup (or anything else).[72]

---

[71]   The title-line of *Didache* is the 'teaching of the Lord via the twelve apostles *to the Gentiles*' (italics mine). Thus the 'hypocrites' of *Didache* 8 are the Jews, and the Malachi quote in chapter 14 arises from that context, although it is being pressed to a direct moral use, with an only marginally less direct application to the eucharist..

[72]   This is relevant particularly to the illustration of the cleansed leper in *Dial*. 41 – if it is pressed, then the individualistic and 'lay' nature of the ex-leper's offering must be noted (see also p.44 below). But Justin's peculiar choice of this as a type of the eucharist, though occasioned by the use of bread, concentrates on the response of thanksgiving far more than on the ritual transaction.

Later authors also applied Mal.1.11 to the Christian dispensation, but, losing sight of its anti-Jewish apologetic use, were divided as to what the Christian 'sacrifice' might be.[73] Perhaps the easy, if unscriptural, identification of the 'pure sacrifice' with the eucharist was always tempered by the knowledge that the only sacrifices the New Testament expects believers to offer are the responsive giving of themselves (Rom.12.1-2), giving of praise and thanks to God through Christ (Heb.13.15) and giving of goods to others (Heb.13.16). A further significant feature of Justin's eucharistic exposition is that, although he insists that Jesus is the high priest after the order of Melchisedek, he does *not* do what later writers cannot resist, and connect Melchisedek's provision of bread and wine (Gen.14.18) with the 'sacrifice' of the Christian eucharist.

(ix) Anamnesis

'*Anamnesis*', provisionally translated as 'remembrance', occurs at intervals in Justin. It comes in the direct quotation of Jesus' words of institution in *Apol*.66 – 'Do this in remembrance of me'. The word comes from Jesus (1 Cor.11.24,25), with only one other direct usage in the New Testament (Heb.10.3). Justin uses it artlessly as a word of ordinary speech, without any sense of defining some sacramental position over against error, or of conveying some technical sense of it to Trypho or to the emperor. He also uses *anamnesis* in non-eucharistic contexts.[74] In both kinds of context the meaning remains close to our 'remembrance', and there is little or no ground for forcing a meaning of 'reminding others' upon it. It occurs in each of the three passages in the *Dialogue* which have explicit eucharistic reference (*Dial*.41,70 and 117), and in each Justin states that the remembrance is specifically (though not exclusively) of the salvific death of Christ.[75]

---

[73] Thus Irenaeus, quoting Malachi, expounds the sacrifice as being the eucharist, but in a harvest thanksgiving role of the offering of the firstfruits (*Adv.Haer*.IV.17); Tertullian says Malachi's 'pure offering' is 'the ascription of glory and blessing and praise' (*Ad Scapulam* III.22); Michael Green further cites Jerome and Eusebius to the same effect ('The New Testament and the Early Fathers' in J.I.Packer (ed), *Eucharistic Sacrifice* (Church Book Room Press, 1963) p.74), while Richard Hanson multiplies further instances from Tertullian (*Eucharistic Offering in the Early Church* (Grove Liturgical Study 19, 1979) p.11), and stresses how *Didascalia* 9 contrasts our offering 'prayers, petitions and thanksgivings' with (Jewish) 'former sacrifices' (*id*.p.15). Edward Kilmartin, in his weighty *The Eucharist in the West* (Pueblo, 1995), a book overtly devoted to charting the history of eucharistic sacrifice in the West, does not even have an entry for 'Justin' in his index, and shows virtually no dependence in later doctrines of mass sacrifice upon either Justin or Mal.1.11 (save that 'puram hostiam' emerges in the Roman rite, and is alleged by the Council of Trent (Sess.22, cap.1) to fulfil, *inter alia*, the Malachi prophecy).

[74] See *Apol*. 44 ('[God] always urging the human race to effort and remembrance, showing that he cares and provides for them') and *Dial*.27 ('[God] summons you to the remembrance and knowledge [of your wickedness]').

[75] In *Dial*.70, where the bread is said to signify the incarnation, even there Justin adds adjectivally that Jesus suffered for us – and the cup signifies his death anyway.

G. A Possible Scenario

Justin portrays a pattern of church life which is simply a 'one-off', saying nothing of other contemporary or future liturgical practice. This is confirmed by the story of his martyrdom.[76] Without exaggerating evidence, we could infer that this learned Christian philospher is in an assembly which meets at the Timiotinian bath on Sundays. It has a leader to name the Holy Tinity over baptismal candidates and to teach and preside at the eucharist; but the choice of leader may be for a limited period only, and the assembly treats itself as corporately celebrating both baptism and the eucharist. The leader is probably accountable to the assembly, on whose behalf he supervises a distribution of food and sustenance to the needy by the assembly's appointed servants, who also take eucharistic elements to the absent. The people ('we') fast and pray alongside baptismal candidates in their preparation and administer the baptism. In the eucharist the people pray together, mutually share the kiss of peace, assent corporately to the thanksgiving, participate in receiving the elements, and physically support one another. Jesus Christ alone is their high priest, and they function in a 'congregational' mode of church life, without duties to Christians or congregations elsewhere.

There is no hint of a bishop or other Christian leaders or congregations in the text.[77] Justin's claim that 'all' who live in the city and around (*Apol*.67) come to the Sunday eucharist sounds pan-Roman; but few imagine he describes the only Christian assembly in Rome, and his answer at his martyrdom suggests just the opposite. But was an author from an isolated congregation competent to make the petition on behalf of the faith to the emperor? Justin's apologetic style is confident, even authoritative, but his writings survive through the high repute in which he was later held by Tatian and Irenaeus, as a mainstream, perhaps the definitive, apologist. That might be odd if he were from a minor Christian offshoot, but for them the orthodox force of his writings was strongly confirmed by his own martyrdom, perhaps eclipsing his ecclesial context. So his relationship to the Christians in Rome at large – bishop included – remains obscure.

---

[76] See p.32 below, and Martin Stringer's exposition quoted in the commentary.

[77] Bradshaw reflects on the apparent distance in space and in culture between Justin and what we might have expected of other Christian assemblies in Rome: 'Since Justin was himself Syrian in origin, and had been baptized at Ephesus, he would have belonged to a community in Rome that was primarily Eastern in membership and would not necessarily have been very familiar with what went on in other Christian assemblies in the city...' (*Eucharistic Origins*, p.64). This speculation (and it *is* speculation) begs questions about whether, in that Greek-speaking Christian context, there then existed any conscious 'Eastern' and 'Western' cultural or liturgical division between neighbouring assemblies in one city – but it highlights the problem of how representative of Christianity in Rome generally, let alone across the Roman world, we can take Justin to be.

2. Texts with Commentary

A. General Worship

APOLOGY

13. What sensible person will not admit that we are not atheists, since we worship the Creator of this universe and assert, as we have been taught, that he has no need of bloody sacrifices, libations or incenses. But we praise him with the best of our power by word of prayer and thanksgiving for all our nourishment. We have been instructed that the only worship of him is not to consume by fire those things which he created for our sustenance, but to employ them for the good of ourselves and the needy, and to offer by our word to him solemn prayers and hymns in our gratitude for our own creation, for the preservation of our health, for the variety of things, and for the changes in the seasons, and bring to him our requests that we may rise again in incorruption because of our faith in him. Our teacher of these things is Jesus Christ, who was born for this end, and who was crucified under Pontius Pilate, procurator of Judaea, in the reign of Tiberius Caesar. We shall prove that we worship him with reason, since we have learned that he is the Son of the living God himself, and believe him to be in the second place, and the prophetic Spirit in the third. For this they accuse us of madness, saying that we attribute to a certain crucified man a place second to the unchanging and eternal God, the Creator of all things, but they are ignorant of the mystery that lies herein. To this mystery we entreat you to give your attention, while we explain it to you.

---

prayer and thanksgiving] Geoffrey Cuming said the passage was 'dealing with the eucharist (or possibly the agape)' (*JTS* 33 (1980) p.81), and he was perhaps inferring that from what is in common here with *Apol.*65 and 67.

all our nourishment [*eph' hois prospherometha pasin*]] Literally, in the passive, 'all things with which we are supplied'.

solemn prayers] The uncommon Greek word *pompai* elsewhere means 'processions' or 'solemnities', but here the verbal offering of them to God suggests some verbal (even 'liturgical') ritual. If he does imply the eucharist, a developing formal character of the sacrament may be concealed under this term.

hymns] Justin does not mention singing in his accounts of the eucharist; but, if this account does include the eucharist, this would suggest songs (whether Psalms or specifically Christian songs) might be used then, making those accounts less than exhaustive at least in this respect.

THE MARTYRDOM OF THE HOLY MARTYRS

2. Rufinus the prefect said 'Where do you assemble?'

Justin said 'Where each one chooses and can: for do you fancy that we all meet in the very same place? Not so; because the God of the Christians is not circumscribed by place; but, being invisible, fills heaven and earth, and everywhere is worshipped and glorified by the believers.

Rusticus the prefect said 'Tell me where you assemble, or into what place you collect your followers?'

Justin said 'I live above one Martinus, at the Timiotinian bath; and during the whole time (and I am living now in Rome for the second time) I am unaware of any other meeting than his. And if anyone has wished to visit me, I have communicated to him the teaching about the truth.'

Rusticus said 'So are you then a Christian?'

Justin said 'Yes, I am a Christian.'

...do you fancy that we all meet in one place?] Martin Stringer reads Justin as saying 'Christians do not all meet for worship in one place in Rome, but rather worship where they choose and where they can.' (*A Sociological History of Christian Worship* (Cambridge, 2006) p.45). If so, Justin's disclaimer of knowing of other gatherings, with his assertion that Christians are free to assemble elsewhere and do so, may indicate a reticence about others at this point when he is under hostile examination, and, if so, is an honourable departure from the transparency of the *Apology*. But it sharpens the questions about how typical his account is of worship elsewhere in Rome when he writes, let alone across the whole Roman Empire over many decades.

B. Baptism

(i) The Circumcision Antecedent

DIALOGUE

14.₁. Therefore through this bath of repentance and the knowledge of God, which has come to be on account of the lawlessness of God's people, as Isaiah cries, we have believed, and we make it known that the only means to cleanse those who have repented is that very baptism which he announced, that is, the water of life. But the cisterns which you have dug for yourselves are worn through and useless to you. For what is the need of that baptism which cleanses the flesh and body alone? ₂. Have your life baptized from wrath and from covetousness, from envy, and from hatred; and, lo! the body is pure. For this is the symbolic significance of unleavened bread, that you do not commit the old deeds of the evil leaven.

---

that very baptism which he announced] In *Dial.*13 Justin quotes Is.53 at length, stating that Isaiah was not directing the people to a literal bath, but to faith in the blood of Christ. Thus his allusions to Is.1.16 are probably metaphorical, without having actual Christian baptism in view.

cisterns] The allusion in chapters 14 and 19 to 'broken cisterns which hold no water' (Jer.2.13) also seems metaphorical. The original texts refer to quenching thirst, but Justin's use is about water for washing, tangentially about baptism. He cites the circumcision of the heart (cf. Deut. 30.6; Jer.9.25-26), which is found among the physically uncircumcised, whether the Gentiles of his own time, or the pre-Abrahamic men of Gen.1-11. Both here and in *Dial.*43 (below) he likes to juxtapose baptism and circumcision (cf. Paul's use in Col.2.11-12). But he does not spell out any continuity from one to the other, nor indicate what uses are metaphorical.

have your life baptized] Literally Justin says 'Be baptized in respect of your *psuche*' – the *psuchen* being an internal accusative. Translating *psuche* as 'soul' raises more problems than it solves (while Trypho's use of it in *Dial.*4-6 looks near a Platonist understanding, Justin does not accept it). As in the New Testament (where, eg, see Matt. 2.20, John 15.13, Rom.13.1), the English 'soul' fastens far more anthropological baggage upon the author's thought than the Greek necessarily implies. See also *Dial.*41 on page 34 overleaf.

19.2. This circumcision is not, however, necessary for all men, but for you alone, in order, as I have already said, that you may suffer these things which you [Jews] now justly suffer. For we do not receive that useless baptism in cisterns, as it has nothing to do with this baptism of life. It is for this reason also God has announced that you have left him, the living fountain, and dug for yourselves broken cisterns which can hold no water. 3. Even you, who are circumcised in the flesh, have need of our circumcision; but we, having the latter, do not require the former. [And Adam, Abel, and Enoch pleased God without circumcision]

28. [We are to be circumcised in the heart] 4...But if someone is a Scythian or a Persian, but has the knowledge of God and of his Christ, and keeps the eternal righteous decrees, he is circumcised with the good helpful circumcision, and is a friend of God, and God rejoices in his gifts and offerings...

29.1. Let us glorify God, the Gentiles gathered together; for he also has visited us. Let us glorify him through the king of glory, through the Lord of hosts. For he has granted his favour to the Gentiles also; and he receives our sacrifices more agreeably than yours. What reason have I then for circumcision, when I have been attested by God? What need have I of that baptism, who have been baptized with the Holy Spirit?

41.4. Further, the command of circumcision, bidding you always to circumcise the children on the eighth day, was a type of the true circumcision, by which we have been circumcised from deceit and evil, through him who rose from

---

circumcised with the good helpful circumcision] A distinction between literal and metaphorical circumcision here seems clear, and in *Dial*.43 literal baptism is either the equivalent of metaphorical circumcision, or the means to it. However, *Dial*.29 is more cryptic, and it is unclear whether 'that baptism' is literal circumcision (which, from the tenor of the argument, it ought to be, and, if so, it provides a strong link in Justin's thought-patterns) or even, as Lukyn Williams affirms (*Justin Martyr: The Dialogue with Trypho* (SPCK, 1930) p.57), proselyte baptism. It is also unclear whether 'baptized with the Holy Spirit' includes literal water-baptism or not.

Let us glorify God] This passage from *Dial*.29 is repeated in a fuller context in the eucharistic texts – see p.43 below.

Further, the command] This passage from *Dial*.41 is also repeated where the whole chapter comes on pages 44-45 below.

bidding you] The 'you' is supplied. 'Us' or 'them' could equally be supplied, providing differing nuances.

him who rose from the dead on the first day of the week] The identifying the first day of the week is discussed on pages 15-17 above. Without mention of baptism, the linking of literal circumcision's eight days with the resurrection of Christ as a 'type' of the true circumcision has baptism only just out of sight (see page 17 above).

understand therefore the stone knives as his words] a delightfully strong metaphor to expand 'circumcision of the heart'.

the dead on the first day of the week, Jesus Christ our Lord. For the first day of the week, remaining the first of all the days, is further called the eighth according to the count of all the days of the cycle, and yet remains the first.

43.2. And we, who have approached God through him [Christ], have received not carnal but spiritual circumcision, which Enoch and those like him observed. And we have received it through baptism, since we were sinners, by God's mercy; and all men may equally obtain it.

113.6. ...circumcised... with knives of stone, namely, the words of our Lord Jesus.... 7. And we shall understand therefore the stone knives as his words, by which so many who were in error have been circumcised from their uncircumcision, with the circumcision of the heart...

114.4. ...our circumcision.. through sharp stones, that is, through the words which have come to us through the apostles of the chief corner-stone, the one cut without hands, and he circumcises us from idolatry and frankly all wickedness.

(ii) Some differing allusions

DIALOGUE

39.2. Therefore, in the very way that God...[see extract from ch.39 on pp.38-39 below]...and are leaving the path of error; who are also receiving gifts, each as he is worthy, enlightened through the name of this Christ. For one receives the spirit of understanding, another of counsel, another of strength, another of healing, another of foreknowledge, another of teaching, and another of the fear of God.

---

enlightened [*pephotismenoi*]] In *Apol*.61 Justin explains that the washing of baptism is called 'enlightenment' (*photismos*)(see also *Apol*.65 below). As he uses the same verb and verbal noun in the *Dialogue*, it seems likely that the *phot-* stem used in *Dial*.39 and (five times) in *Dial*.122 refers to baptism. In *Dial*.39 the coupling of the name of Jesus with enlightenment looks overwhelmingly baptismal, and that use reinforces the understanding of *ematheteuthesan* as including baptism (see page 38 below). This mirrors the meaning of *photismenoi* in Heb.6.4 and 10.32, and of *matheteuo* (with overt baptismal reference) in Matt.28.19 and, almost as transparently, in Acts 14.21. In *Dial*.122 the citing of Is.42.6 just previously in *Dial*.121 and of Is.49.8 here (cf. Luke 2.32) ushers in the Messiah to 'enlighten', against the inability of the old 'Law' to do so. Baptism is not so directly in sight, but is hardly right out of sight.

86.6. ...and as we have been baptized from the weighty sins which we have committed, Christ has redeemed us, by being crucified on the tree, and by purifying us with water; and he has made [for] us a home of prayer and adoration.

87.1....Trypho said...2. 'Tell me then about Isaiah's word, "A rod shall come out from the root of Jesse; and a flower shall grow up from the root of Jesse; and the Spirit of God shall rest on him, the spirit of wisdom and understanding, the spirit of counsel and strength, the spirit of knowledge and godliness; and the spirit of the fear of the Lord shall fill him."'

---

the Spirit of God shall rest upon him] Baptism is hardly in view in the quotation from Is.11, not least because it is Trypho who quotes it. Without the advocacy which follows here, the passage would not have qualified for inclusion. But E.C.Ratcliff says that Justin has so constructed the *Dialogue* that 'Trypho is nowhere allowed to ask, "If, then, possession of the Spirit makes a man a Christian, when and in what way is the Spirit given to him?"' Ratcliff says the answer could only be given to a catechumen, and not to Jew nor emperor. His desired answer is that the Is.11 extract is known down history in a confirmation context (so could it have originated before Justin talked with Trypho?), and that Luke's account of the baptism of Jesus so visibly separates the baptism from the descent of the Spirit as to make it clear that a two-stage initiation was in Justin's mind (E.C.Ratcliff 'Justin Martyr and Confirmation' in *Theology* (Vol.li, No.334, 1948), reprinted in A.H.Couratin and D.H.Tripp (edd), *E.C.Ratcliff: Liturgical Studies* (SPCK, 1976) pp.110-117). But we note that Is.11 is *not* associated with 'confirmation' in the actual extant 'confirmation' texts of the next two centuries (as, e.g., in Tertullian and Hippolytus), that Justin interprets it to state that all the powers of the Spirit are Christ's and are distributed by him in different ways (far from a confirmation understanding), and also that Justin, in *Dial*.88 on page 37 opposite, separates Jesus' baptism and the descent of the Spirit far less than Ratcliff is stating of Luke. Crucially this *is* speculation, done in the interests of a particular desired outcome. Ratcliff provides a wonderfully transparent move from 'It may not be impossible to hazard a guess' – the modest phrase with which he begins his quest for the predetermined quarry – to his 'Justin's statements...make it appear improbable that Justin regarded water-baptism as the whole of Christian initiation' with which he concludes it. This is equally wonderfully matched by Couratin's own following of Ratcliff, thus 'the initiatory rite known to Justin consisted of Baptism with Water, Anointing with Oil, Prayer for the Descent of the Messianic Spirit and Baptismal Eucharist' (in 'Justin Martyr and Confirmation – A Note' in *Theology* Vol.lv, No.390, 1952). It is further backed by a characteristic trip into typological fantasy-land by Lionel Thornton (*Confirmation: Its Place in the Baptismal Mystery* (Dacre, 1954) pp.39-44), after all of which it is a relief to get back to straight Justin. See also pages 18-19 above, and the commentary on 'one receives the spirit of understanding' in *Dial*.39 on pages 38-39 below.

88.3. ...And then, when Jesus had gone to the river Jordan, where John was baptizing, and when he went down into the water, a fire was kindled in the Jordan; and the apostles of this our Christ himself wrote that, when he came up from the water, the Holy Spirit lighted on him like a dove. Now, we know that it was not because he had need to be baptized, nor for the Spirit to descend upon him like a dove, that he went into the river; just as he had no need to be born and to be crucified, but he did so for the sake of the human race ...[repeated later in chapter]

122.[In ch.121 Christ is 'a light of the Gentiles']₁. ...these words... refer to us who have been enlightened by Jesus...3...[they] also refer to Christ and to the Gentiles who have been enlightened ...4...[some of the Jews cried] 'Surely it refers to the Law and those who are enlightened by it?'... 5 [Justin replied] No...for if the Law was able to enlighten the Gentiles and all who possess it, what would be the need of a new covenant?...we must not understand it of the old Law and its proselytes but of us the Gentiles whom he has enlightened...

138.2. For Christ, the firstborn of all creation, became the point of origin of another race, one regenerated by him through water and faith and wood, which held the mystery of the cross, even as Noah also was saved, when he was borne upon the waters with his family. When therefore the prophet says 'In the time of Noah I saved you', as I said before, he is speaking to the people who were similarly faithful with God, and had these symbols...3...Yet, in that the whole earth, as the scripture says, was flooded, and the water was lifted up fifteen cubits above all mountains, it is clear that God was not referring to your land, but to the people who obey him, for whom also he prepared beforehand a rest in Jerusalem, as also has been proved aforetime by all the symbols of the flood. I say that by water and faith and wood they that prepare themselves beforehand and repent of their sins shall escape the judgment of God that is to come upon them.

---

point of origin [*arche*]] Other translators render this 'head'.

(iii) Infant Baptism?

APOLOGY

15.[Bigamy and lust are alien to Christians] ...many men and women who had been made disciples of Christ from childhood remain pure at 60 or 70 years of age; I am proud to say I can cite examples from every nation. Why should we mention here the countless throng of those who turned from intemperance to learn our teaching? Christ came indeed to call to repentance not the just or the pure, but the impious, the incontinent, and the unjust, for he said 'I came not to call the just, but the sinners to repentance.'

DIALOGUE

39.₁.[God said to Elijah 'I have yet seven thousand who have not bowed the knee to Baal']...₂. Therefore, in the very way that God did not then inflict his anger on account of those seven thousand men, even so in the same way neither has he up to now inflicted judgment nor does he now inflict it, knowing that daily some are being made disciples into the name of Christ himself, and are leaving the path of error; who are also receiving gifts, each as he is

---

had been made disciples of Christ from childhood [*ek paidon ematheteuthesan*]] While baptism is not actually named here, *Apol.*15 was ransacked by Joachim Jeremias in his *Infant Baptism in the First Four Centuries* (ET, SCM, 1960, p.72) to provide evidence of infant baptism. See 'being made disciples' below.

being made disciples [*matheteuomenous*]] The verb *matheteuo* is used in the active in association with baptism and 'into the name' in Matt.28.19, and in the passive by Justin here in the *Dial.*39 passage where 'being made disciples' has a context which, without specifically mentioning baptism, clearly implies it, and the phrase 'into the name' (cf. Acts 19.5, 1 Cor.1.13,15) adds to the case – for early Christian authors could hardly contemplate converts 'being made disciples' on one occasion, and 'being baptized' on another. Kurt Aland, who opposed Jeremias (in *Did the Early Church Baptize Infants?* (ET, SCM, 1961) pp. 71,73), argued that *ematheteuthesan* meant receiving instruction prior to baptism, claiming that *ek paidon* could mean 'from being youths'. Jeremias responded (in *The Origins of Infant Baptism* (ET, SCM, 1963) pp.55-57), propounding a tight link here between *matheteuesthai* and baptism on the one hand, and demonstrating that Justin is contrasting 'cradle Christians', who, when grown, still 'remain pure', with the 'countless throng' of adult converts, on the other. Thus believers who were 60 or 70 years old around 155 AD had been baptized *as infants* within the first century, a very primitive instance indeed. Geoffrey Wainwright warns 'This kind of evidence would admittedly be valuable only as a support to a very strong case' *(Christian Initiation* (Lutterworth, 1969) p.43) – but the case is cumulative within the New Testament, and this evidence does then support it. Children are not mentioned in the actual account of baptism in *Apol.*61 (on pages 40-41 below) – but would they be?

worthy, enlightened through the name of this Christ. For one receives the spirit of understanding, another of counsel, another of strength, another of healing, another of foreknowledge, another of teaching, and another of the fear of God.

---

enlightened [*photizomenoi dia tou onomatos tou Christou toutou*]] See ch.1(E(iii)) on page 17 above.

one receives the spirit of understanding] This sentence partly echoes the passage in *Dial.*87 (see page 36 above). Justin freely combines Is.11.2 and 1 Cor.12.28, but in the process binds the gifts of the Spirit to 'being made disciples' (*matheteuesthai*) and 'being enlightened' (*photizesthai*), both of which elsewhere signify 'being baptized'. Thus this usage rather strengthens the case that Justin's use of Is.11 in *Dial.*87 differs totally from its later use in confirmation rites.

(iv) The Baptismal Rite

APOLOGY

61. But the way in which we also dedicated ourselves to God when we were made new through Christ we will explain, lest by omitting it we might appear to err in the explanation. As many as have been persuaded and believe that those things which we have taught and asserted to be true are true, and undertake that they can live in this way - these people are taught both to pray and to ask of God while fasting the forgiveness of their former sins, while we pray and fast together with them. Then they are taken by us to where there is water, and they are reborn with the rebirth by which we ourselves were reborn. For it is in the name of God the Father and Lord of all and of our Saviour Jesus Christ and of the Holy Spirit that they then take the bath in water. For Christ also said 'Unless you are reborn, you will not enter into the kingdom of heaven' - but that it is impossible for those who have been born once to enter back into the wombs of those who bore them is evident to all.

---

dedicated ourselves...persuaded and believe] The baptismal requirement is credal conviction along with moral commitment.

we pray and fast together with them] In the New Testament baptism is universally given within hours or even minutes of a profession of conversion. *Didache* 7 has a brief preparation, and Justin hints here at a more thorough teaching and examining (it is odd to find L.W.Barnard writing 'The catechumenate did not take definite form until c.200C.E.' *(St. Justin Martyr: The First and Second Apologies* (Paulist, New York, 1997) p.101, n.61) as though we had secure negative information for the whole of two centuries about the whole Roman world). Members of the assembly share in the final prayer and fasting, and model a welcoming fellowship. The liturgical sequence then underlines belongingness without ever saying the converts are 'incorporated'.

reborn] This verb, drawn from Jesus' words in John 3 which follow, is a standard characterization of baptism by Justin. See ch.1(E(iii)) on page 17 above.

in the name of God the Father...and of...Jesus Christ...and of the Holy Spirit] While Jesus appears to have given a Trinitarian formula to his disciples (Matt.28.19), we have no evidence they used it formulaicly. The New Testament does, however, consistently present the centrality and, presumably, the power of the 'name' (usually of Jesus Christ) in baptism. The Matthean formula comes in *Didache* 7, and must have been universally known. However, later, in Hippolytus, the candidate answers questions by professing belief in each of the three persons of the Godhead in turn and being dipped once at each answer. This also seems to conform to Jesus' commission, and Justin's wording about 'naming' leaves his practice undefined. His trinitarian focus, repeated near the end of the paragraph, appears accurate for his pre-Nicene times but is not closely formulaic.

take the bath in water] 'Bath' (*loutron*) is a regular word in Justin (*Dial*.14; *Apol*.61,62,66; cf.Titus 3.5). It is tempting to think it is used literally enough to imply submersion – certainly it squares poorly with sprinkling or minimal pouring.

And it was explained by Isaiah the prophet, as we have written earlier, by what means those who have sinned and are repentant shall escape their sins. It was stated by him thus:

> "'Be washed, make yourselves clean, put away the evil from your lives, learn to do well, judge in favour of the orphan and justify the widow; and then come and let us reason together" says the Lord; "and though your sins are as scarlet, I will make them as white as wool, and though they be as crimson, I will make them white as snow. But if you do not listen to me, a sword will devour you." For the mouth of the Lord has spoken this.'

And we have learned from the apostles the reason for baptizing as we do, as follows. We were ignorant of our first birth and were born of necessity from a random seed through the union of our parents with each other, and we developed in shameful and evil ways of life; so, in order not to remain as children of necessity and ignorance, and in order to receive forgiveness for the sins we have previously committed, in the water there is named over the person who wishes to be reborn and repents of his sins the name of God, the Father of all and Lord; and the one who leads to the bath the one who is being washed speaks this name on its own, for no-one can speak the name of the ineffable God – and if anyone dares to say what that name is, he is raving with hopeless insanity. And this bath is called 'enlightenment', as enlightening the understanding of those who are becoming disciples. And the one who is being enlightened is washed also in the name of Jesus Christ, who was crucified under Pontius Pilate, and in the name of the Holy Spirit, who through the prophets announced in advance all that relates to Jesus.

---

explained by Isaiah] The passage from Is.1.16-20 looks like a gift to Justin for expounding baptism.

over the person who] Justin has moved from generalities in the plural to visualizing and reporting how some one person is baptized.

the one who leads to the bath...speaks this name] This 'leader to the bath' is Justin's nearest approach to an officiant at baptism. The leader articulates a question or a formula over the candidate (see above re 'in the name..'), but is not said to administer the water, which Justin says 'we' (corporately) do.

enlightened] The *photiz-* stem comes three times in one sentence, and is equated with 'becoming disciples'. See ch.1(E(iii)) on page 17 above.

(v) Passing Retrospective Allusions

APOLOGY

62.₁. And when the demons heard about this bath...

65.₁. But after we have thus washed him who is persuaded and has assented we bring him to those who are called the brothers...

66.₁. .... 'eucharist', to share in which is unlawful for anyone except whoever believes that what has been taught by us is true, and has been washed in the bath which is for forgiveness of sins and unto rebirth, and is living as Christ commanded.

---

bath] See page 40 above.

after we have thus washed him] 'Washing' is a favourite significance of baptism in Justin, and 'we' are the regular agents of baptism. The assembly is gathered separately (see pages 17, 20 and 40 above), which raises a question about how extensive were the 'we' who had fasted and prayed with the catechumen before his baptism, as well as the 'we' who had baptized him. As Justin identifies himself with the baptismal party rather than with 'the brothers' in the assembly to whom 'we bring' the newly baptized, does this indicate anything of his own role?

is living as Christ commanded] This reads as though some who were baptized could be disqualified – i.e. excommunicated – from communion if their lives showed evidence of backsliding or apostasy. This exactly parallels *Didache* 9.

C. Eucharist

DIALOGUE

28.4.[Wherever someone has circumcision of the heart,] God rejoices in his gifts and offerings. 5. But I will provide for you, my friends, words of God himself also, when he spoke to the people through Malachi, one of the twelve prophets. These are the words:

> "'I have no pleasure in you", says the Lord; "and I will not accept the sacrifices at your hands: for from the rising of the sun to its setting my name is glorified among the Gentiles; and in every place a sacrifice is offered to my name, and it is a pure sacrifice: for my name is honoured among the Gentiles" says the Lord, " – but you profane it."'

And through David he said 'A people whom I have not known served me; at the hearing of the ear they obeyed me.'

29.1. Let us glorify God, the Gentiles gathered together; for he also has visited us. Let us glorify him through the king of glory, through the Lord of hosts. For he has granted his favour to the Gentiles also; and he receives our sacrifices more agreeably than yours. What reason have I then for circumcision, when I have been attested by God? What need have I of that baptism, who have been baptized with the Holy Spirit?

---

through Malachi] These two chapters contain Justin's first citation of a prophecy which he reckons very powerful against Trypho, namely Mal.1.11-12 (he returns to it in *Dial.*41 and *Dial.*116 and 117 – see ch.1(F) above and the passages below). It is a proof-text that the Old Testament itself foretells a Gentile dispensation to outstrip the contemporary Jewish one in its worship's acceptability to God. The 'sacrifices' (*thusiai*) are not here expounded, let alone identified as the Christian eucharist, but are merely asserted as belonging to the Gentiles.

a sacrifice] Justin misquotes Malachi slightly here: the original (and the Septuagint) say 'incense (*thumiama*)...and a pure sacrifice (*thusia*)', but Justin has 'sacrifice (*thusia*)..and [*or* even] a pure sacrifice (*thusia*)'. Justin may be (carelessly?) misquoting, but he knows the correct text, for he quotes it in *Dial.*41 (see below). So has he bowdlerized it here, using the repetition of *thusia* to diminish the sense? Or is it a scribal error of transcription – where a hand which began a word with '*thu-*' has, through some reflex inadvertence, gone on to *thusia* rather than *thumiama*? An alternative explanation would be Justin's aversion from 'incense' (see *Apol.*13 on page 31 above), the material associated with emperor-worship and anathema to Christians; but, if Justin actually amends Malachi's text, his misquoting gives a hostage to Trypho on the one hand, and will shortly be rendered useless by his correct quotation in *Dial.*41 on the other.

Let us glorify God] The same passage occurs in the baptism section on page 34 above.

41.₁. And the offering of fine flour, sirs (I said), which was prescribed to be presented on behalf of those purified from leprosy, was a type of the bread of the eucharist, which our Lord Jesus Christ prescribed for us to do in remembrance of the suffering which he endured on behalf of those who are being cleansed in their lives from all evil, in order that we may at the same time thank God for having created the world, with all things that are in it for the benfit of humanity, and for delivering us from the evil in which we had our being, and for destroying the principalities and powers with a final destruction through him who became subject to suffering according to his will. ₂. Hence

---

offering of fine flour] Justin returns to the theme of Jewish sacrifices with a double Old Testament reference. First comes the response of the cleansed leper in Lev.14.1-32, where the grain offering was part of the ritual follow-up to the cleansing. Justin, with both the idea that the eucharist is a 'sacrifice' (see Ch.1(F(viii)) above), and the sense that becoming Christian is a cleansing, presses the typology upon Trypho. The heart of it is the thanksgiving of the leper, which is matched, says Justin, by our thanksgiving for not only creation, but also our own deliverance from evil, a close antitype, we infer, of cleansing from leprosy. The levitical 'type' has, of course, severe limitations, as the cleansing *motif* and once-only restoration ritual suggest a closer comparison to baptism, and the 'fine flour' has but a very minor role in Lev.14. Ratcliff worked this up (even drawing upon the 'eighth day' in the Leviticus account, not mentioned by Justin) as part of his 'lumping' thesis which connected Justin with Hippolytus (see 'The Cleansed Leper's Offering before the Lord: Edward Ratcliff and the pattern of the Early Anaphora' in Bryan Spinks (ed*) The Sacrifice of Praise: Studies...in honour of Arthur Hubert Couratin* (CLV, Rome, 1981) pp.161-177 – but Spinks is not aligning himself with Ratcliff). Justin surely makes a passing speculative comparison, one not only somewhat implausible in itself, but also not adopted or quoted by any other extant author? We do not learn how convincing Trypho found it.

in remembrance [*eis anamnesin*]] *Anamnesis* is employed by Justin as a key to the purpose of the eucharist – in *Apol.*66 he quotes Jesus as saying 'Do this in remembrance of me *(eis ten anamnesin mou)*' and he here becomes the first extant author since the Gospel-writers to relate 'anamnesis' to the eucharistic celebration, as he is here the first since them to connect the eucharist with the death of Christ (see Ch.1(F(ix)) above).

lives [*psuchas*]] See the commentary on *Dial.*14 on page 33 above.

God speaks by the mouth of Malachi, one of the twelve [prophets], as I said before, about the sacrifices at that time offered by you:

"'I have no pleasure in you" says the Lord; "and I will not accept your sacrifices at your hands; for, from the rising of the sun to its setting, my name has been glorified among the Gentiles, and in every place incense is offered to my name, and a pure offering: for my name is great among the Gentiles" says the Lord "but you profane it.'"

3. And he is speaking in advance of the sacrifices offered to him by us Gentiles in every place, that is, the bread of the eucharist, and similarly the cup of the eucharist, saying both that we glorify his name, and that you profane it. 4. Further, the command of circumcision, bidding you always to circumcise the children on the eighth day, was a type of the true circumcision, by which we have been circumcised from deceit and evil, through him who rose from the dead on the first day of the week, Jesus Christ our Lord. For the first day of the week, remaining the first of all the days, is further called the eighth according to the count of all the days of the cycle, and yet remains the first.

---

mouth of Malachi] The second Old Testament reference is the Mal.1.11-12 text, already cited in *Dial*.28 (as Justin mentions) and due again in 116-117. The text differs slightly from the ch.28 quote – 'incense' (*thumiama*) is restored, conforming properly to the Septuagint. Justin's purpose is the same – to distinguish Christians from Jews in the economy (and favour) of God. But this time he expounds the sacrifice of the Gentiles as true worship offered at the eucharist. Again, the actual purpose in offering the bread and cup to God, having no scriptural basis, remains elusive.

Further, the command] This part of the chapter is also on pages 34-35.

eighth day] See pages 15 and 17 above. Justin is more clever than convincing in linking the eight days from birth to circumcision to the day of Jesus' resurrection.

70.2. [Isaiah says]'...12.Whoever walks in righteousness, speaking a right way, hating lawlessness and unrighteousness, keeping his hands away from bribes, stopping his ears from hearing the unjust judgment of blood, closing his eyes from seeing unrighteousness, this one shall dwell in a lofty cave of a strong rock. Bread shall be given to him, and his water shall be sure...' 15. It is plain therefore that in this prophecy there is reference to the bread, which our Christ gave to us to eat in remembrance of his being made flesh for the sake of those who believe in him, on whose account he also suffered, and to the cup which he gave us to drink with thanksgiving in remembrance of his blood.

Bread...water] This quotation from Is.33 provides a 'food and drink' theme to enable Justin to say it is a prophecy fulfilled in the eucharist. His expounding of 'water' with 'bread' as being of the eucharist assisted the Harnack proposal that Justin reports a bread-and-water eucharist. See ch.1(F(iv)) above.

...in remembrance...in remembrance] For '*anamnesis*' see page 29 above. There is an interesting (almost latterday) division between the bread being a reminder of the incarnation and the cup a reminder of the crucifixion (see ch.1(F(ix)) on page 23 above).

116.3. ...we are the true high priestly race of God, as God himself bears witness, saying that in every place among the Gentiles they are presenting to him well-pleasing and pure sacrifices. Now God receives sacrifices from no one, except through his priests.

117.1. So God, anticipating all the sacrifices which Jesus Christ provided should be done through that name, that is, those which are done by Christians in every place of the earth in the eucharist of the bread and the cup, bears witness that they are well-pleasing to him. But he disavows those done by you and through those priests of yours, when he says, 'And your sacrifices I will not accept at your hands; for from the rising of the sun to its setting my name is glorified' he says, 'among the Gentiles - but you profane it.' 2. Yet right up to now, in your love of contention, you assert that God does not accept the sacrifices of those who dwelt then in Jerusalem, and were called Israelites; but that the prayers of the people of that race then dispersed he says do please him, and that their prayers he calls sacrifices. Now, that prayers and giving of thanks, when offered by worthy people, are the only perfect and well-pleasing sacrifices to God, I also admit. 3. For these alone Christians also have undertaken to offer, and they do so in the remembrance

---

true high priestly race of God] Sacrifices to God have to be offered by priests. But a direct contrast emerges between 'those priests of yours' and the whole 'race' of Christians, who are the 'true' priests, corporately fulfilling the role contrasted with that of the Jewish priests of Malachi's time. See also ch.1(D(iii)) on pages 13-15 above.

presenting to him well-pleasing and pure sacrifices] The Mal.1.11 allusion in ch.116 is followed by a larger extract in ch.117. Although there is a double reference to the eucharistic 'bread and cup' and 'solid and liquid food' in ch.117, the overall teaching here is that the 'prayers and giving of thanks' by Christians, offered supremely *at* the eucharist ('in the remembrance effected...'), are the true sacrifices that are 'well-pleasing and pure' and fulfil the Malachi prophecy. This is confirmed by the mention of nomads etc offering 'prayers and thanksgivings' at the end of ch.117 without reference to any sacramental context, and by the longer wording of 'true and spiritual praises and thanksgivings', again with no sacramental context, in ch.118.

'I will not accept...'] This quoting of Mal.1.11-12, following closely on the extract in ch.116, is part of the recurrent advocacy towards the Jew. Here it is truncated, and not open to a checking against the Septuagint and the wording in chs.28 and 41.

in the remembrance] For *anamnesis* see ch.1(F(ix)). The simple genitive used of the food has an interesting subjective role, unlike the usual objective genitive naming of the thing or person being remembered.

effected by their solid and liquid food, in which the suffering which the Son of God endured on their behalf is remembered. His name the high priests and teachers of your people have caused to be profaned and blasphemed through the whole earth. But those filthy garments, which have been put by you on all who have become Christians by the name of Jesus, God will reveal as taken away from us, when he raises all from the dead, and appoints some to be incorruptible, immortal, and free from sorrow in the everlasting and imperishable kingdom, but sends others away to the eternal punishment of fire. 4. But because you and your teachers are deceiving yourselves when you interpret what the scripture says as referring to those of your nation then in dispersion, and maintain that their prayers and sacrifices offered in every place are pure and well-pleasing, learn that you are speaking falsely, and trying by all means to cheat yourselves; for, first of all, not even now does your race extend from the rising to the setting of the sun, but there are nations among which none of your race ever dwelt. 5. For there is not one single race, of barbarians, or Greeks, or whatever they may be called, nomads or vagrants or herdsmen living in tents, among whom prayers and thanksgivings are not offered through the name of the crucified Jesus. And then, as the scriptures show, at the time when Malachi wrote this, your dispersion over all the earth, which now exists, had not taken place.

118...2...and on his [Christ's] second advent do not suppose that Isaiah or the other prophets are speaking of sacrifices of blood or of libations being presented at the altar, but of true and spiritual praises and thanksgivings...

---

is remembered] Other translators render 'brought to mind' – but the *mnem-* stem (here without the *ana-* prefix) is best translated consistently as 'remember'. Neither the Greek nor the English have to imply that the person remembering had been present at the event remembered, though the Christian use perhaps implies an element of entering into what is remembered...

your dispersion] Justin departs from the regular comparison of the sacrifices offered, and (surely lamely?) seeks to show that Malachi's prophecy could not have been fulfilled among the Jews *because they had not expanded far enough*!

APOLOGY

65.₁. But after we have thus washed him who is persuaded and has assented, we bring him to those who are called the brothers, where they are gathered together, to make common prayers earnestly for themselves and for the one who has been enlightened and for all others everywhere. We pray that having learned the truth we may be counted worthy to be found both good citizens by our works and keepers of the commandments, in order that we may be saved with the eternal salvation. ₂. We greet each other with a kiss, when we have ceased from the prayers. ₃. Then there is brought to the president of the brothers bread and a cup of water and wine mixed with water; and he takes these and lifts up praise and glory to the Father of all

---

after we have thus washed] The narrative runs in sequence to ch.61 (see p.41 above), though divided from it in the *Apology* by three chapters about pagan aberrations, and here eucharistic texts are separated from baptismal ones.

make common prayers] This is where the pattern common to the 'Sunday' eucharist (ch.67 below) begins. It is slightly fuller here, and Justin refers back to it in ch.67 as his basic account. Within the sentence Justin passes from the third person ('they') to the first person ('we') as the party from the baptism, with which he identifies, joins the gathered assembly. The prayers are intercessory and comprehensive, but include in passing the newly baptized convert as fully part of the assembly, and show a concern (for the emperor's benefit?) for Christians to live as 'good citizens', before an eschatological conclusion. For the issue of who was articulating the prayers (and with what freedom) see ch.1(F(iii)) above.

greet...with a kiss] Although the kiss only comes in this account, it does not centre on the new convert, but is rather the mutual greeting of the congregation. The initiatory kiss of the bishop to the newly baptized in later rites is unlike the mutuality here (though Edward Phillips says that its presence here, and its absence in the Sunday account, 'may be significant' (L.Edward Phillips, *The Ritual Kiss in Early Christian Worship* (Alcuin/ GROW Joint Liturgical Study no.36, Grove Books, 1996) p.22)). See ch.1(F(ii)) above.

president] The responsibility passes here from the congregation to the person of the president. For his status as president see ch.1(D(iii)) above.

bread and a cup of water and wine mixed with water [*kai kramatos*]] The 'bringing in' and the 'mixed cup' are discussed in ch.1(F(iii)) above. The 'and wine mixed with water' are missing from the Codex Bobbonianus, which gave rise to speculation discussed in chapter 1. It *is* a curious expression, but that does not justify following the poor manuscript.

takes these] The 'taking' (*labon*) could possibly mean 'receiving', to complement the bringing in by others, but, as the verb used of Jesus himself in the Gospels and 1 Cor.11, it is more natural to see it as a direct echo from these accounts, a taking up of the elements, the first 'dominical act'. It differs from Christ's actions in uniting the treatment of both elements. The brief mention of 'taking' is omitted in *Apol*.67, a further instance of this chapter providing the fuller account.

lifts up [*anapempei*] praise and glory] Does this 'sending up' prefigure the 'Lift up your hearts' of later years?

things through the name of the Son and of the Holy Spirit; and makes thanksgiving at some length that we have been counted worthy of these things from him. When he has completed the prayers and the thanksgiving, all the people present respond, saying, 'Amen'. 4. Now the 'amen' in the Hebrew language means 'Let it be so'. 5. Then, when the president has given thanks and all the people have responded, those who are called by us 'deacons' provide for each of those present to share in the eucharisticized bread and wine and water; and for those who are not present they take some away.

___

worthy of these things] The Greek has *touton*, 'these (things)'. Some have translated it 'gifts' or 'favours' which may be appropriate, but are sharper-edged than Justin's pronoun.

'deacons'[*diakonoi*]] These distributants of communion may represent an 'order' of deacons, but are just as likely to be less defined 'servants' of the assembly, and the inverted commas indicate Justin's explanation to the emperor.

they take some away] It looks as though they are going that day to people's homes, nearer to our 'extended communion' than 'permanent reservation', so that the recipients share at a distance in that day's eucharist.

66.1. And this nourishment is called by us 'eucharist', to share in which is unlawful for anyone except whoever believes that what has been taught by us is true, and has been washed in the bath which is for forgiveness of sins and unto rebirth and is living as Christ commanded. 2. For it is not as common bread and common drink that we receive these, but as Jesus Christ our Saviour, having become flesh by the word of God, took both flesh and blood for our salvation, so also we have been taught that the nourishment which has been eucharisticized through the word of prayer which comes from him – nourishment by which our blood and flesh are nourished by transformation – is both the flesh and blood of the Jesus who became flesh. 3. For the

___

And this nourishment...commanded] This is included with comment in the last baptismal section (see page 42 above).

to share in which is unlawful] This provides the theme – the chapter's teaching about the eucharist is there to report the restricted participation in the central activity of the assembly, excluding those not qualified.

flesh and blood] As the sentence begins with a Johannine account of Jesus' incarnation (from John 1.14), so the Johannine 'flesh' is the natural word for him to use of the significance of the eucharistic bread. In John's Gospel and Epistles 'flesh' has high dignity signifying full human physicality without shortcomings, and John attributes 'eucharistic' words to Jesus with 'Unless you eat the flesh of the Son of man...' (John 6.53). In Paul, on the other hand, 'flesh' regularly denotes fallen nature. 'Flesh' is the constant rendering of the *sarx* stem here, even where in other places 'incarnate' might be used, to exhibit the consistent use of stem in three different contexts.

eucharisticized through the word of prayer which comes from him] See ch.6(F(v)) on pages 24-25 above for a discussion of both the translation and the implication of this phrase.

apostles in the memoirs which were produced by them, which are called 'Gospels', delivered in this way that it had been commanded to them: that Jesus took bread, gave thanks, and said 'Do this in remembrance of me: this is my body'; and similarly took the cup, gave thanks, and said 'This is my blood'; and he shared it with them alone. 4. And this in the mysteries of Mithras the evil demons also imitated this and commanded that it should be done; for that bread and a cup of water are provided, along with certain formulae, in the ceremonies of initiation you either know or can learn.

Jesus took bread] For the place of the narrative in Justin's argument, see ch.1(F(vi)) above. While the institution of the Lord's Supper is here traced to the Gospels, Justin's actual wording looks closer to 1 Cor.11.23-26 – not least in the adverb 'similarly' (actually *hosautos* there, but *homoios* here in Justin) and the famous '*eis ten anamnesin*'. However, an oral tradition of the institution, whether or not within the eucharistic liturgy, could well have been attributed to 'the Gospels', even if textually owing more to the Pauline account.

'Do this in remembrance...'] See ch.1(F(ix)) on page 29 above for a wider discussion of *anamnesis*.

mysteries] This word Justin uses of pagan rituals; his only Christian employment for it is to say in *Dial.24* that the eighth day has a 'mystical meaning'.

67.1. But after these events we always thereafter remind each other of these things. And those of us who have possessions help all those who lack them, and we always remain with each other. 2. And for all things that we eat we bless the Maker of all through his Son Jesus Christ and through the Holy Spirit.

---

these events...these things] The Greek 'these' stands without nouns in both cases – perhaps meaning 'after the ceremony of being baptized and sharing in communion...we remind each other of the meaning of these'.

those...who have possessions help] This mutual help not only echoes Acts 2.42-47, but also establishes Justin's assembly as a gathering of people who love each other and form a supportive community.

we always remain with each other] This again seems to imply a common life far beyond simply meeting on Sundays.

for all things that we eat] cf. 1 Tim.4.4-5

day...called 'Sun-day'] See ch.1(D(iv)) above. Justin adds his reasoning from the resurrection of Christ later in the chapter. The time of day the gathering occurred is not clear, though the Roman term, 'Sun-day', precludes any possibility of Saturday night. As Justin insists that the Sunday eucharist matches the baptismal one, it is unlikely they were at different times from each other; and the two accounts perhaps read more naturally as referring to a morning gathering than to an afternoon or evening one.

an assembly of all] It is difficult to set limits to Justin's 'all' – does he mean 'all believers' or 'all who belong to my assembly' or some other 'all'? 'All' in any case cannot be exhaustively literal as it has to be qualified by mention of the absent a few lines below. Peter Lampe says Justin here 'describes a typical liturgy in a house-church community as a pattern that takes place everywhere in the world on Sundays' (*From Paul to Valentinus, op.cit.p.365*), and Justin's second use of 'all' lower down perhaps supports that interpretation.

3. And on the day which is called 'Sun-day' there is an assembly of all who live in the cities or the fields, and the memoirs of the apostles or the writings of the prophets are read as long as time allows. 4. Then, when the person reading has stopped, the president in an address gives instruction and encouragement to imitate these good things. 5. Then we all rise together and make prayers; and, as I mentioned before, when we have ceased from praying, bread and wine and water are brought in, and the president in the same way offers up prayers and thanksgivings, according to his ability, and the people assent by saying 'Amen'. There is both a distribution to each and a sharing in the eucharisticized elements, and a sending to those not present by the means of the deacons. 6. Those who are well off and willing give each what he wishes according to his own purpose, and what is collected is deposited with the president. 7. It is also he who helps both orphans and widows, and those who lack through illness or another cause, and those who are in chains, and visiting strangers; and in short he has the responsibility for all who are in need. 8. Now we all hold our common assembly on Sun-day, because it is the first day, the day on which God changed the darkness and matter when he made the world; and Jesus Christ our Saviour rose from the dead on the same day. For it was on the day before Saturn's that they crucified him, and on the day after Saturn's, that is, Sun-day, that he appeared to his apostles and disciples and taught them these things, which we have also handed on to you for your consideration.

---

memoirs of the apostles] See *Apol*.66 above, where these are identified as the 'Gospels'. See also on 'the president...address' below.

writings of the prophets] Almost certainly the Old Testament scriptures. See also on 'the president...address' below.

the president in an address] This, with the readings of scripture, apparently constitutes our 'ministry of the word' – the first time we have a clear indication of this shape to the rite. It forms a single block, which, as noted earlier, is only reported of this Sunday eucharist, though it *may* have marched in parallel with the baptismal rite as the congregation awaited the newly baptized (see ch.1(E(ii)) above). After it the congregation 'rises', which suggests they were seated or reclining during the ministry of the word.

as I mentioned before...in the same way] Justin emphasizes that he is summarizing here what he told in fuller detail in *Apol*.65.

those who are well off and willing] Justin does add here some information beyond the *Apol*.65 account – a practical outworking of love and mutual support springing from the assembling together. For the president's role and standing see ch.1(D(iii)) above.

all hold our common assembly] See 'an assembly of all' on page 50 opposite.

on Sun-day] Here is the rationale for the first day of the (Jewish-Christian) week. See ch.1(D(iv)) on pages 15-16 above.

3. Some Modern Implications

Anglicans have always been ready to assert the importance – and the authority – of 'the early church'. Cranmer of course invoked a supposed pattern of 'the early Fathers' in his Preface to the 1549 and 1552 Prayer Books (reprinted as 'Concerning the Service of the Church' in 1662), but he was there discussing daily lectionaries, and his treatment of sacraments and other rites showed neither interest in ancient uses nor dependence upon them, but solely a concern to be biblical and clear. However, his Preface gave excuse for the sub-committee on liturgical revision at the 1958 Lambeth Conference to issue the mind-boggling prospectus:

'It was Cranmer's aim to lift worship in England out of the liturgical decadence of the late medieval Church...and to recover as much as possible of what he called the "Primitive Church". In this he achieved notable success, but there was not available in his day the historical material necessary for the full accomplishment of his aim. Since that time, and indeed since 1662, valuable evidence has been brought to light, by the use of which what he began may be further developed.'

The questions begged by this prospectus are threefold:
1. Was Cranmer truly seeking to follow second or third century uses?
2. If he was, was he right to do so?
3. If he was right, and we are pursuing patristic models, then do we truly have access to relevant further material to fill out deficiencies in the picture he had?

The evidence is that Cranmer was *not* seeking to follow early church models[78]; and our own conclusion must be that, even if we wished to follow them, the evidence we have is so slender as to be nearly invisible. However good a camera-shot we may get of Justin's liturgical practice, it is amounts to no more than one camera-shot in one part of one city at one point in time in a period of more than a hundred years of what is otherwise almost entirely unrecorded Christian practice. And, as a matter of fact, the camera-shot is not always clear – for Justin was not addressing our questions, and failed to focus on much that we would like to see more clearly. But if we accept or skirt those limitations about Justin, and instead hypothesize that 'the early church' is to be located in the third or fourth

---

[78] That is not to say that he would not cite patristic evidence to show his traditionalist opponents that their own insistence that their uses were in continuity and conformity with the early church was unsustainable in the light of the evidence. Bradshaw, *The Search, op.cit.*p.x.

centuries (let alone in the *Apostolic Tradition* of the supposed Hippolytus), then, although we may have marginally more evidence on which to go, it is neither consistent with itself nor adhering to scripture, nor obviously in developing sequence with that camera-shot from Justin.

The advocacy of following 'the early church' flourished in the years following Lambeth 1958. It fuelled the Church of England Liturgical Commission in the early 1960s, not only on the grounds that 'the early church' had authority in how we should worship, but also on the seductive thesis that this quest would get us 'behind the Reformation' and its doctrinal divisions, and instead deliver us into a peaceful sphere of agreed, authoritative and unifying forms of worship. This was either self-deluding or actually deceitful. The archetypal early church worship which was sought quickly reduced to a subjective outcome of modern scholarship. The apologia that using primitive forms was a unitive procedure often concealed the actually partisan character of what was being drafted, leaving Anglicans the hard task of getting back to debating issues on the grounds of biblical doctrine, rather than chasing the will o' the wisp of 'the early church'.

We can still acknowledge helpful models in the slender patristic evidence we possess. In today's Anglican liturgies we have reunited the profession of faith with the administration of the water of baptism, we have incorporated baptism into the eucharist, we have begun to play down confirmation as integral to that process, in the eucharist we have located the intercessions to follow the ministry of the word, we have placed the peace between the intercessions and the eucharistic action, we have prepared the table immediately before starting the thanksgiving, and we have viewed the thanksgiving and the distribution as *the* constitutive elements of the eucharist. Each of these mirrors the evidence of Justin; Justin has provided a fruitful model and precedent to which our revisers have referred.

But a model, however helpful, is not an over-riding authority. The proviso stands that the Bible has to have supreme authority over all later traditions, and we cannot draw upon a particular early author uncritically, simply on the grounds that he is early. The quest for *authoritative* primitive models for our liturgy is itself a mistaken process, both as a matter of principle and in terms of any available outcome. A serious study of Justin on his own terms confirms Paul Bradshaw's judgment 'many of our previous confident assertions about "what the early church did" now seem more like wishful thinking or the unconscious projections back into ancient times of later practices.' But the study may still enrich.

The Alcuin Club
promoting liturgical scholarship and renewal

Eucharistic Origins
by Paul Bradshaw
a challenging account of what can and cannot be known
about the origins of the Eucharist
(SPCK 2004 - ISBN 0-281-05615-3 - £17.50)

House of God: House of the People of God
by Robin Gibbons
a creative exploration of how liturgical space
shapes the worshipping community
(SPCK 2006 - ISBN 0-281-05762-1 - £14.99)

Christian Prayer through the Centuries
by Joseph Jungmann
a new English translation of a liturgical classic
(SPCK 2007 - ISBN 0-281-05759-7 - £9.99)

The Companion to Common Worship (two volumes)
edited by Paul Bradshaw
a detailed discussion of the origins and development
of each Common Worship rite
together with a comprehensive commentary on the text
(Volume 1, SPCK 2001 - ISBN 0-281-05266-2 - £19.9)
(Volume 2, SPCK 2006 - ISBN 0-281-052778-8 - £19.99)

Celebrating the Eucharist
by Benjamin Gordon-Taylor & Simon Jones
a popular and practical guide to the celebration
of the modern Eucharistic rite
(SPCK 2005 - ISBN 0-281-05588-2 - £9.99)

The Use of Symbols in Worship
edited by Christopher Irvine
an account of the history of the liturgical use of
water, oil, light and incense
together with a practical guide
to using these symbols today
(SPCK 2007 - ISBN 0-281-05852-5 - £9.99)

To order any of these titles, or for details of how to join the Alcuin Club,
email alcuinclub@gmail.com or telephone 01745 730585.
For all full list of Alcuin titles, go to www.alcuinclub.org.uk
Generous discounts available to members.

Alcuin/GROW Joint Liturgical Studies

48-56 pages, £5.95 in 2008. Nos 1-58 by Grove Books Ltd, Ridley Hall Road, Cambridge CB3 9HU

*Nos.4 and 16 are out of print. Nos 59 and following are published by SCM-Canterbury
– see outside back cover*

Grove Liturgical Studies

*These Studies of 32-40 pages ran in 1975-86, and are published or distributed by
Grove Books Ltd. Price in 2007, £2.95
Titles omitted are out of print.*

Grove Books Ltd, Ridley Hall Road, Cambridge CB3 9HU   Tel: 01223-464748
www.grovebooks.co.uk